NORTH

TWEEDSMUIR
PROVINCIAL PARK

Bella Coola

◄ Lonesome Lake

BRITISH COLUMBIA

VANCOUVER
ISLAND

Vancouver

U.S.A

PACIFIC
OCEAN

Victoria

Fog swamp

Living with Swans in the Wilderness

Trudy Turner
Daughter of Ralph Edwards, "Crusoe of Lonesome Lake"
& Ruth M. McVeigh

hancock

house

ISBN 0-919654-63-0

Cataloging in Publication Data

Turner, Trudy, 1929-
Fogswamp

Autobiographical.
ISBN 0-919654-63-0

1. Turner, Trudy, 1929-
2. Trumpeter swan. 3. Birds, Protection of -
British Columbia. I. McVeigh, Ruth M.
II. Title.
QL31.T87A3 598'.41'0924 C77-002022-4

LCC 77-5181

FIRST PRINTING 1977
SECOND PRINTING 1978

Published simultaneously by

Hancock House Publishers Ltd.
3215 Island View Road
SAANICHTON, B.C. V0S 1M0

Hancock House Publishers Inc.
12008 1st Avenue South
SEATTLE, WA. 98168

CONTENTS

1   Anahim Lake-Lonesome Lake.
    Friday, February 13, 1976   7
2   Growing Up at Lonesome Lake   13
3   The Trumpeter Swans   19
4   How The Swans Were Saved   37
5   Lonesome Lake, February 14, 1976   45
6   Establishing Fogswamp Farm   59
7   Trails and Roads   81
8   Lonesome Lake, February 15, 1976   89
9   Weather and Watermelons   95
10 Voices of the Wild   105
11 Jack and the New Yorkers   109
12 Bathing Bears and Growling Grizzlies 117
13 Furred and Feathered Neighbors   123
14 Fire!   141
15 Floods and Other Disasters   149
16 Vigorous Vacations   195
17 Fogswamp Horse Sagas   213
18 Cow Problems and Problem Cows   225
19 "People-Watching" in the City   239
20 Williams Lake, February 20, 1976   245

DEDICATIONS

To my loving husband Jack and daughter Susan who washed the dishes while I typed.

Trudy Turner

To my family, particularly my Mother, for a lifetime of encouragement.

With thanks to my Dad and daughter Barb for constructive criticism, to Gerry, who freely let me go (and the Turners, who let me come!)

Ruth McVeigh

1

Anahim Lake - Lonesome Lake
Friday, February 13, 1976

"It's snowing like Billy-be-damned," a voice shouted outside my motel window first thing this morning. As an opener to a day on which weather was crucial if I was to realize my long-standing dream, it left something to be desired, but even though my first reaction was panic, nothing could subdue my eagerness to be up and doing. I leapt from bed and peered out at fast-falling flakes as the significance of the date, Friday 13th, hit me. This was the day I was scheduled to fly out to Lonesome Lake to meet the Turner family with whom I was to spend a week or so.

As with thousands of other readers who have read *Crusoe of Lonesome Lake*, my imagination had gone winging when I read Leland Stowe's fascinating story. His book, written in 1957, told the exciting story of Ralph and Ethel Edwards who carved a pioneer life out of the wilderness and raised three children in the splendid isolation of British Columbia's Coast Chilcotin country. It was their daughter Trudy and her family I was on my way to visit.

With boundless optimism I got organized to leave and went over to the cafe for breakfast. The skies cleared enough for a flight just about the time I finished my second cup of coffee after lunch, so I said goodbye to the friendly and helpful folk of Baxter's and was driven out to the airport.

First glimpse of the tiny Beaver made me gulp. It looked so fragile against the backdrop of endless country stretching toward the Coast Range. The pilot stowed my gear aboard and we roared down the runway, banking enough after take-off for me to catch a final glimpse of Anahim Lake. Being very inexperienced at flying in small planes, I found comfort in looking out the windows and noting what a short distance it seemed to the treetops! Then I glanced out the opposite side and could scarcely believe the depth of the chasm through which the Atnarko River flowed far, far below. Ten minutes or so later, I glimpsed the flat expanse of ice which covered Lonesome Lake.

We circled the Turner place in the recognized signal for the arrival of visitors. Way down in the little toy farmyard a tiny figure could be seen running toward the house. Soon three people were standing in the field, looking up at the plane.

We put down about four in the afternoon. The pilot took off again as soon as my baggage was unloaded, leaving me feeling more solitary than ever before in my life. The stretch of frozen lake and the silent, forest-clad mountains seemed to comprise the entire world.

While waiting for the Turners to arrive, I decided to walk up to the original Edwards homesite. As I puzzled over the best route to the house, a tall man with bushy grey hair, huge beard and delightfully gentle twinkling blue eyes greeted me. I learned this was Stanley, the Edwards' eldest son. His soft voice gave no hint of his own slight deafness. I asked for Mrs. Edwards so he led me to the kitchen door and introduced me to his mother. She was working at the stove, amid a clutter that obviously represents what happens when folks live half a century in circumstances which make them reluctant to dispose of anything. Even if it's not currently in use, there's always the chance it might come in handy. The small house contains souvenirs of all the multi-faceted people who lived and grew up there, together with gifts and communications from people all over the world. Mrs. Edwards, now in her seventies, is a tall slim woman who had clearly been a beauty in her youth. She lives alone in the cabin doing far more work than she can really cope with, even with the assistance of Stanley and occasionally her other son John, both of whom live nearby. Her husband Ralph left the area almost a decade ago to operate a fishing boat in the Prince Rupert district. He is now retired and lives at Oona River.

Mrs. Edwards' main interest is her cows, raised for home consumption as well as for the beef which provides a good part of the limited annual income. She is very fond of the animals and much prefers tending a newborn calf to being indoors cleaning house. The farm itself seems to have just evolved and lacks the organization which would make it easier to manage. Ralph Edwards would appear to have been a man of vision and big ideas, challenged by the goal of making his mark on the territory, the complexities of developing a sawmill and the 'impossibility' of building and flying his own plane. On the other hand, he probably just couldn't see the inconveniences which plagued the everyday running of his household.

After signing the guestbook, I returned to the hangar just in time to see the Turner clan emerge from the woods at the end of the ice. Trudy, Jack, their daughter Susan and I introduced ourselves to one another and made preparations for the walk to their place. Roping as much of my gear as possible on their packboards, they led off on the mile-and-a-half trail through the woods to their farm at a gait I dubbed the Lonesome Lake lope! Shouldering my own pack, and having been assured that Friday 13ths are lucky at Lonesome Lake, I followed.

Impressed by the spectacular scenery and the rushing river's musical accompaniment, I couldn't resist asking Trudy how on earth she came to give the place its dour name— Fogswamp Farm. Her reply provided some insight as to her method of dealing with upsets as well as a hint of just how stubborn she might be.

The original name given to the pre-emption when she took it up in 1951 was Seven Islands, for the group of small islets in the Atnarko River where it flows through her land. A few years later in the course of developing her property, she was felling trees, accompanied only by the very first dog she had ever owned. Just as the tree began to topple, Trudy saw that Pup lay directly in the path the unpredictable, dead, dry alder was going to fall. Trudy yelled "timber!" The dog understood the term and got up but there wasn't time to get clear. The tree killed her instantly. Trudy mourned the loss of her dog by re-naming the farm with the dreariest, most depressing name she could dream up. So it became

Fogswamp Farm. Everyone begged her to reconsider but by then she had made up her mind and her decision became firmer with every protest.

By the time Trudy had explained the origin of the farm's name, we were approaching the outbuildings. Rail and snake fences surrounded a collection of neat log buildings. Pushed back only a short distance beyond the fences were thick woods where towering firs and clumps of birch mixed with other trees and undergrowth. In all directions mountains loomed over the insignificant mark which domesticity had made on the valley. We went through a couple of creaky gates and entered the main compound which contained the barn, smokehouse, woodshed, outhouse, root house, meat safe and the five-room cabin.

A small snow-filled corral piqued my curiosity since it had no gate or opening. Seems the Turners have an ingeniously efficient method of planting ready-fertilized apple trees— they feed their cows apples! The log corral enclosing a fifteen foot square area contained a "volunteer" which got its start this way but sprouted on such poor soil it was decided not to transplant it but simply to protect it from browsing animals. As we progressed further, I noticed two of the cows looked most peculiar. The smaller one was wearing a rawhide bag over her muzzle to prevent her eating stuff she shouldn't get into. The slightly bigger one wore around her muzzle a rawhide band with a ring of spikes set into it. This, I was informed, was to make the mother discourage her calf from nursing. Taking a horrified look at the sharp points which would encounter the mother's belly if her youngster tried to get a drink, I muttered, "I should think *so*" and reached a sympathetic hand out to Mama Valerian. Like the other farm animals, she was very shy as they rarely see strangers. All the cows, plus the huge bull Domino, reacted as though I had dire plans for them, rolling their eyes as they backed away.

As we reached the house, Trudy said she would show me where I could put my bedding and other baggage. I was escorted to my very own accommodation, a small log structure built twenty years previously by Trudy. I made my bed of air mattress and sleeping bag laid over the rough plank floor and returned to the Turner cabin about three hundred feet distant. After a scrumptious steak supper and some conversation, I persuaded young Susan to walk me to my quarters. I didn't know what terrors the short walk might hold, but I felt I wanted company for it! As she left, I undid the laces on the cowhide which served as a door, fastened them again on the inside and stood quietly as the silence engulfed me. The cowhide triggered a memory of a fragment of suppertime conversation as we were enjoying the well-flavored beef. "Well," said Trudy, "Domino and that cow you're eating..." The rest of the sentence got lost as my mind boggled. I'd just never thought of my supper on quite such personal terms! With a relaxed chuckle I decided to get to bed.

The small lantern threw shadows on the log walls as I slipped into the icy sleeping bag. I doused the light and suddenly was utterly alone in the dark, surrounded by miles of untamed forest. The only sound was the distant rush of the river and a faint whisper in the trees above the roof. My cowardly self ardently hoped it would hear nothing more than that as I began to get warm in the down-filled bag and reviewed the opening hours of my adventure.

I visualized the young woman who had built the cabin so long ago and thought about the older Trudy I had just met— vital, vibrant, but not quite as I had imagined when I first read about her. She is shorter and a little stockier than I had pictured. She wears her hair short as a man's for convenience and has expressive bright blue eyes and a slightly prominent nose. Her manner is that of an alert small bird, cautious and wary but still extremely curious and interested. My last thoughts were of the next morning when Trudy would begin to tell me in her own words the story of her family's arrival in the lovely valley and something of her own life . . . . . .

2

Growing Up at Lonesome Lake

In August of 1912, my father, then a young man, was on his way up the Atnarko valley, seeking land with lakes and mountains. He met three brothers who had pre-empted quarter sections along the fertile banks of Stillwater and one of them agreed to guide him to a long, narrow lake where there was arable land.

Leaving Stillwater, the pair followed Goat Creek for several miles, then climbed to the 3500-foot flat occupied by the Turner Lake chain of wood-rimmed waters. When they arrived on the west shore they constructed a heavy raft of pine logs which they paddled across the lake. They then continued overland to the top of the slope to Lonesome Lake, a distance of about two miles. Not knowing a better way, they plunged straight downhill, circumnavigating rock outcrops and clambering over windfalls, coming out near where we now feed the swans, a descent of 2,000 feet.

After looking over the piece of land on the east side of the head of Big Lagoon and agreeing it was worth applying for, the two men turned back down Lonesome Lake, as it was later named by my father.

It was late summer when Dad discovered the land he wanted. By the following January he had received his pre-emption. He came right back in, with 600 pounds of supplies. I understand this freight was horsepacked to Stillwater, where it was boated to a place where he and his trapper friend back-packed it a further three miles to Lonesome Lake. They then built a sled and hauled the whole load up the frozen surface, a distance of five or six miles.

In 1908 my mother was a four-year-old who had moved with her family from Alberta to the Bella Coola valley. They had been wheat farmers who were hailed out once too often and decided to try their luck in a new part of the country. She grew up in Bella Coola and in 1923, when she was nineteen, she and my father were married. They had met in the course of his trips out to pick up mail. Together they established themselves over the years, developing a farm they called The Birches and raising me and my two older brothers, Stanley and John.

I was born in a log cabin without benefit of professional medical assistance and have never known any home but the isolated fastness of Coast Chilcotin in British Columbia.

My father was pretty much of an authoritarian, reserving his respect for things that worked and people who did, too. His own inventiveness, tenacity and plain hard work enabled our family to live in almost total independence. His conviction that dogged determination plus imagination and energy could overcome any obstacle, infected all of us. I was the youngest of the trio and reputedly inherited my father's "got to know" compulsion. From the time I was old enough to be able to contribute my physical energies to getting chores done, I was expected to do so. Even as a small child I was given the jobs of milking cows and training them to lead.

My eldest brother Stanley headed for "outside" when he was just seventeen, encouraged by my parents who felt the boys deserved the right to select their own life styles. Two years later John departed for a taste of more refined living, so by the time I was thirteen, I had pretty well developed into my parents' "right hand man".

I never had much companionship from my brothers and was always rather a loner, although I never considered I was alone since I had the horses. My first conscious memory is of sitting on a bay mare named Topsy. I was about three at the time and recall I was on the horse's back through my own insistence. Riding horses was what I enjoyed most as a youngster. That, and feeding the beautiful swans which have had a profound influence on the entire course of my life.

I grew to love the wild environment very early and developed a kinship with it. It has never been my way to pit myself against the forces of nature but rather to try to ally myself with them. Since the wilderness has been my environment since birth, I am far more adapted to it than to civilization's jungle. When I was only a small child I grew interested in the trumpeter swans and still enjoy them and find them fascinating. I learned to imitate the calls of many of the wild creatures around my home and generally am successful in eliciting a reply. I respect animals and their ways even if they do not always do what I would choose.

By the time I was fifteen, I was considered by my family to be a pretty capable ranch hand, able to take care of myself in the woods and to do my share on pack trails. I was also learning a great deal about trumpeter swans.

My childhood was filled with hard work and study combined with some fun and battles with my brothers and a close companionship with the four-footed and winged creatures around the farm. Nevertheless, it was a strange sort of life, being the only girl child for miles in every direction. I never knew what it was to have a close friend of my own sex and as my school lessons were outlined and marked in Victoria I missed the give-and-take of a classroom. Although I don't recall any really close talks with my parents when I was a little girl, I was always pretty well aware of the facts of life. They're pretty hard to escape on a farm unless you keep your eyes closed and I don't tend to do that.

I began correspondence school at the age of eleven and went through grades four and five in the first year. Then, because of having so much time taken up with farm chores, I slowed to one grade per year. Formal schooling stopped at Grade 9, although I started some Grade 10 courses. Of course, the correspondence school work did not comprise the total intellectual stimulation to which I was exposed. I grew up with books and truly cannot remember ever being unable to read. Both my parents were avid readers and there were always lots of periodicals around the house including *Saturday Evening Post, Time, Reader's Digest, National Geographic,* various farm papers and two or three women's magazines. From the time I was ten the radio was an important focal point through which the family received current news of happenings outside the valley.

There were literally hundreds of books on the shelves at The Birches. Every cent my father could spare was always

15

spent on books. Even after a fire wiped out our first home and everything in it, he immediately began to re-stock the library. A wide assortment of books on mechanical subjects, volumes which provided the family with information on all aspects of our surroundings, sat side by side with texts on the arts, philosophy, music and a well-worn Webster's Unabridged Dictionary. Reference works on plant identification, bacteriology and other scientific matters were well above my head when I first explored them but I delved into them anyway, puzzling out as much as I could. There was also a collection dealing with one of my father's passions—airplanes. It is a matter of record that he came close to building his own plane through technology learned entirely from books. The dream was never realized only because it would have been too complicated and risky to put that much money into a project which might well have been turned down by the Department of Transport. I recall building lots of model planes with my father but to the best of my recollection they never flew very far.

The family got its own airplane, just the same. In 1953 I went to Vancouver to take flying lessons. Those few months spent in the city were pretty harrowing since I had never before been out of the wilderness. I lived at the home of family friends and submerged myself in studies and the challenge of flying. After successfully completing the examinations, I then had the job of selecting and purchasing the plane my father and I had dreamed of and planned for so long. Then I simply flew the plane from the field at Vancouver, home to Lonesome Lake, which for some reason people seem to find an astonishing feat.

The following year my father went out and got his flying licence and the problems of joint ownership of the plane began. I had done all the flying the first year, but after my father got his own licence, we shared the job of delivering produce from The Birches to various camps and resorts in the region which included Charlotte and Nimpo Lakes. I didn't particularly like the fact my father tended to take over the flying, only permitting me to do it under the most ideal conditions. I chafed at the restrictions and lost some of my initial enthusiasm.

During my brief flying career I had much pleasure and a few tense moments. Once when returning via Knight Inlet from a trip to a coastal logging camp, the ceiling closed down over the Klinaklini River and since there is a long stretch there with no fit place for a plane to land, I flew back to Knight Inlet and landed there. I ran into trouble on the same route a few days later but that time had flown so far through the pass there was no possibility of turning back when a solid wall of grey fog suddenly materialized, completely enveloping the Taylorcraft and cutting off all visibility. The little plane could fly herself if trimmed properly and the controls not moved. The pass was only about 500 to 1000 feet wide—not much room for error—but it was also short. Twenty-five seconds later I came out of the fog still on course with the clear blue Pacific far below. I had sat completely still, unable to see a thing. At 80 m.p.h. one travels a fair distance in half a minute!

Another time, on a return trip from Bella Coola, the weather was clear but there was a gale blowing down the Talchako River. At about 5,000 feet we hit extreme turbulence, apparently caused by the wind hitting the rock wall on the north side of the valley and mixing with a strong west wind. It was so rough I seriously considered the chance the wings might be ripped off. The plane climbed at a rate of several hundred feet a minute, then suddenly dropped a thousand feet or more, only to jolt to a sudden stop and begin climbing again. The fragile little craft was being shaken like a rat by a savage dog. Because the wind and turbulence were so severe, it seemed to take an eternity to fly ten miles. Once past the mouth of the Talchako River, the air was smooth and the remainder of the flight was uneventful.

Fog and mist are unpredictable. One time a white sheet seemed spread over the valley where Lonesome Lake lay but when I got close enough I could see a half-mile opening into which I was able to sideslip. I levelled out and put power on again only about 300 feet above the water. I had to fly at that altitude or lower all the way to the landing. Another morning I was going to head for Nimpo Lake but everything except Lonesome Lake was swathed in a vast white fluffy blanket. The fog lay over all the Turner Lake basin and only the peaks thrust their ice-wreathed heads above it. I wanted to stay there, circling like an eagle in an updraft, but feared the fog would close, so returned to earth.

Nearly all the flying I ever did was during the summer and fall of 1953 but during that time I logged more than 200 hours on the plane and developed a real affection for the Taylorcraft seaplane CF-HEO. Some ten years later the little craft suffered an ignominious end on a gravel bar in the outlet of the Bella Coola River. I never flew her after 1958 because it became too difficult to plan the sharing of the schedule with my father. The plane underwent several operations, including an engine and fusilage transplant after it tipped the first time and sustained salt water damage.

As a young woman I always had it in my mind to make a home and a life entirely on my own but I did cherish the hope that through some magic I would find a partner. Still it never occurred to me that I mightn't be able to make a living on my own land, independently. I figured I'd probably raise and sell beef. In any case, I'd make out. I learned a great deal from my parents and their way of life, some of which I later drew on for guidance but other aspects I discarded as being in conflict with the kind of life I wanted. One thing I knew for sure—I wanted my very own place.

At the age of twenty-one, I rebelled against living at home. A few lots in the valley had been surveyed in the early 1900s. I selected the one most arable and sent my application in to pre-empt the land. A short time later I became owner of 160 acres, one-and-a-half-miles south of my parents' place. There I began to build my life.

The first thing I tackled was an 8 x 14 foot cabin to be constructed out of small cedar logs. It took just three days to put up the walls and roof of my little abode. The work was done entirely by me with the help of my horse which hauled the logs and lined them up. They were only small, about eight inches at the butt. I did have help falling the huge cedar tree from which the shakes for the roof were made.

As soon as I finished the cabin, I hacked out a rough road and with some help, built a seventy-foot-long bridge, the third span ever put across the Atnarko. Since it crossed a very narrow place in the river, it was called the Venturi Bridge.

As the months passed, I slowly cleared land and even made some hay. Since I was working alone with only hand tools, it did not seem to me that the results of my labors were very significant. The period until 1957 was an extremely busy one for me, as I was working at my parents' farm when needed, keeping my cows at my own place and feeding the swans throughout the winters.

18

3

The Trumpeter Swans

The landing call of the rare and beautiful trumpeter swan shattered the stillness of a Christmas card day in late December as I neared the place where these large white birds receive their meager rations of grain.

The thermometer stood at 32°F below zero when I left the house for the "swannery" on December 29, 1968.

It was not warm in the house, either! Frost which had formed between the planks and the cowhide on the floor squeaked and crunched as we walked across it even though we had kept the Ashley heater blasting all night. Lighting the cookstove in the kitchen warmed the floor enough that it at least stopped squeaking but water remained frozen in pans on the floor just a few feet from the heater.

Thirty-two below is cold for here and the dog, which had not felt lower temperatures than about 20 below, considered the house the best place for her. We had gone only about 100 feet when she sat down and attempted to get all four feet out of the snow at once! She had been able to make the distance to the barn when I fed the stock and milked the cow but she apparently considered five miles in such temperature as being entirely too much. I relented and sent her back to the house, then started off for the spot where the north end of Big Lagoon joins the river which then flows into the head of Lonesome Lake. It is here we feed the trumpeter swans each winter.

For several days the temperature had dropped a little lower each morning, until it hit bottom. My mother had called on the two-way house phone that morning to report a temperature two degrees even lower at her house, one-mile-and-a-half closer to the swans' feeding place.

Despite these extreme temperatures the ice of Big Lagoon was rotten. Only along the shore where the weight of snow had caused the ice to crack, allowing water to run over the top and melt the snow into slush, had it frozen thick enough to walk on. The crust was still breaking in places near spring holes and there was water on the ice wherever snow remained. Even sub-zero temperature can't freeze water through a two-inch insulation of snow.

As I plowed along the partly broken trail toward the swans' feeding station, my footsteps made no sound and an impression of stillness dominated the frozen valley. This was punctuated by sharp and frequent reports of pine and birch trees splitting from the ever-increasing internal pressure of their frozen sap.

The feedplace, still in the shadow of the mountain to the east, was deserted except for a few dozen shivering white humps far down the channel. The humps silently awaited sunrise, their heads under their wings, their feet tucked up into the thick feathers under their bodies. The rest of the trumpeters apparently had sought a warmer spot and perhaps some open water for the night.

Some distance from the sleeping swans, I noticed the wide, staggered tracks of a large, late-roaming grizzly which had gone wallowing off through the unbroken snow towards the mountain, after following the trail for awhile.

The sun and I were racing each other to the feedplace and I could see the sun would win. I expected the other swans would start showing up and sure enough, at that moment, I heard them. Those on the ice answered in low notes, barely raising their heads out of their shelter.

The sun was just emerging above the jagged, snowclad crest of Mt. Ada, casting long shadows across the ice where it glistened and sparkled on the crystallized surface of the snow.

A pair of swans came in then, high over Lonesome Lake, contrasting brightly against the brittle blue of the northern sky. The sun made them appear pristine, although on the snow they show up creamy-white.

They continued high until over the feeding grounds when they folded their wingtips steeply down and extended their big webbed feet to lose lift. Spiraling down to the ice, they made a swishing roar somewhat like a distant jet. They immediately stretched their feet out behind themselves, shaking off adhering particles of snow, then tucked them up into the warm feathers of their bellies. Then they, too, became humps.

All the river channel was frozen except for a very narrow opening, revealed by a slowly rising column of steam. I would feed the swans there and they would climb out on the ice around the hole to get grain scattered on it, breaking down the edges and thus enlarging the area of open water.

Only about a third of the eventual total arrive at the lake in the fall. Their numbers gradually increase until late January, with most of the increase occurring after it becomes necessary to begin feeding. We count the swans every day in order to see how much grain to dispense. When the flock is small, counting is not too much of a problem but when there are 400 of them the job can get complicated! If they are standing on the ice, we count the forest of necks, adding or subtracting as swans get up and change positions. However, when they are milling around in a bathtub-sized pool, all we can count are the cygnets and even that is not easy if they are crowded together too closely.

These huge birds live in flocks most of the winter and at feedtime rub shoulders with one another to get the grain. There is a small area, where the ice forms last, where we feed them and they all crowd and shove trying to get the grain before some other swan does. They seldom fight over food although occasionally one swan will lift another's neck out of the water if it happens to be where that swan wants to eat! Often one bird will grab the feathers on another's neck and pull and tug only to have the persecuted swan jerk its head out of the water and go after the prodder. Mostly they just push and reach. When they get excited the swans on the far side of the flock push so hard they force some of the birds right up against the feeder's legs. Sometimes while eating grain, one will reach its long slender neck over another's so that when the bottom one comes up for air, the two two-foot-long necks become tangled. Both swans pull and the necks separate, at which point the swans resume eating, dredging grains from the river bottom.

These big birds cannot dive. They must eat in water no more than three feet deep. They tip up on end, paddle furiously to stay upside down for about two minutes, then up come the heads and down go the rumps.

A full grown swan weighs close to 30 pounds and is about five feet from the end of his short tail to the tip of his long black shovel of a bill. When he stands up on the ice he is around four feet tall, head up. Their wings span about seven feet from tip to tip and are at maximum a foot wide. All that is black on the adults are their bills, eyes and feet. The cygnets are a gray-brown color with black-gray-yellow or pink splotched feet and black, pinkish or yellowish bills.

When I began feeding the swans years ago, they would hiss at me whenever I moved to throw out grain at a different spot. Through the years they have learned I don't plan to harm them and now they seldom hiss. They are very timid and any sudden or unusual motion startles them and they will all fly away, leaving their grain, if scared.

Back in 1950 there were only about 80-90 trumpeters so when the feedplace froze up I could chop out a hole for them to eat in. For one six-week period the average temperature in the morning was -16°F. The feedplace froze up each day and all the other water was frozen everywhere. At the north end of Big Lagoon there are relatively warm springs that kept the ice thin and I chopped these out each day for the swans. The ice thickened daily until it got to be eight inches around the hole and each day I was chopping out three inches of new ice, shovelling the pieces onto the surrounding ice. As soon as the hole was free I threw the feed in so the birds could eat before it froze over. New ice began forming immediately.

Some swans became so tame that winter they would lie on the ice around where I was working and I had to be careful not to throw broken ice on the closest ones which were sleeping, heads under their wings. The cygnets were the tamest. I remember in particular a young one which would, lie on the ice about six feet from where I was chopping, sleep for a few minutes, open one eye and look around a bit, then go back to napping. When the feedhole was ready for grain that tame youngster would waddle the six feet to the hole, slide into the water and swim across to me as soon as I began to open the sack. Then the young bird would reach his long neck up and take grain right out of the dish or directly from my hand.

Each day the ice took over a little more of the holes by thickening around the edges. Finally I used a cross-cut saw to cut the ice connecting the holes. Even this didn't bother them as they appeared to think whatever I did to the ice was all right.

The lowest temperature I ever recall was -46°F. That morning felt mighty cold and only a dozen swans came for breakfast. The others must have flown out to the coast where it was warmer. They returned the following day. Three days after that frigid one the mercury had risen to a tropical 46 above and it was raining hard.

I don't know what temperatures in the Chilcotin district were that winter but when it was 32 below at Lonesome Lake in December, we heard on the radio that it was -60°F at Anahim Lake only 26 miles northeast of us.

When that long cold spell started, a north wind blew steadily for a day-and-a-half at about 40 miles an hour, then quit. The sky cleared to a brittle blue and the mercury began its downward trip. It must have gone lower than this area had experienced for a long time as it killed a lot of the native trees. The whistling swan cygnet that was trying to winter with the trumpeters died, too. They apparently are not made for such cold weather as several have tried to winter here but invariably die before spring.

There are too many swans now for us to break ice for them as it took me about two hours to make a hole for just eighty birds. We have not had such a severe winter since, and the problem would not be as great even if we did. There are so many swans they can generally break the ice to create their own hole. Even if they can't, it is no longer so important as they have learned to eat the grain off the ice. Two hundred swans have a combined weight which can sink and finally break two inches of clear water ice, if the flock can be bunched closely enough. We get them to do this by throwing the grain on the ice in a concentrated area. They all crowd around it, the ice begins to sag and splits into large pans as clear as window glass and about as brittle. The swans eat the grain, then shove the large ice pans away down the river under the other ice and the hole stays open for a short time.

Graceful in flight, stately on the water, they are about the clumsiest walkers you could ever expect to see. They waddle along, never paying any attention to what they are walking over or on. They slide on glare ice and sit on their rumps. They trip and stumble over lumps or ridges and often manage to tread on their own huge feet. They don't go around a hummock. They just flop and straddle their way over it, looking off in the distance somewhere!

They can attain a speed of 50 miles an hour with their strong though relatively slow wing-beat, their necks undulating almost imperceptibly from the effort of moving those impressive wings. They usually take off and land into the wind like airplanes. Their landings are stylish. A whole family will come in, power off, wings bent down at the tips until they are a few feet above the water. They then throw up their big webbed feet, put on a little power and slide onto the surface of the water on the heels of their feet and tails. After sliding on the surface like a hydroplane for ten feet or so, they settle down on their breasts, neatly fold their wings and paddle off, looking very pleased with themselves. They use the same technique when landing on ice or snow. They invariably slide gracefully onto a surface instead of plopping into the water with a great spray like a mallard.

The big birds can take off from a standing start if pushed by fear where there is no place to run to get up speed but ordinarily they run and flap their wings for 15 feet or so to get up flying speed. A large flock taking off right in front of a person produces a wind strong enough to blow a hat off and the noise of their wingtips hitting the water and their feet splashing makes a deafening roar that can be heard a mile.

Some swans seem to have a sense of fun. Once when Jack was feeding them he saw one member of a family of swans play with a muskrat. These animals are vegetarians and in no way a threat to a swan. The young cygnet was one of a family of five idly swimming around when he spotted the muskrat sitting on the edge of the ice eating a piece of pond weed. The cygnet swam to within two or three feet of the muskrat and stared at him a few seconds then reached out his long neck and looked the muskrat right in the eye. Unperturbed, the animal went right on eating, so the mischevious swan reached out even further and dabbed the muskrat on his head. At this, the confused 'rat picked up his piece of weed and retreated about three feet back on the ice before continuing to eat. The swan apparently didn't feel like bothering to climb out on the ice to carry on the persecution so turned and swam haughtily away, wagging his tail to and fro in a saucy manner.

Due to the scarcity of the trumpeter swans in North America, the Severn Wildfowl Trust in England decided they should obtain a few of the rare birds. In the summer of 1951 Peter Scott of the Trust arranged with the Canadian government that the swans be made a gift to the-then Princess Elizabeth. During November, R.H. Mackay and D.A. Munroe of the Canadian Wildlife Service flew in to Lonesome Lake and a trap was constructed for the purpose.

The trap consisted of a post and pole framework, covered with seine netting. The entire trap was about 50 feet long by 10 or 12 feet wide and around seven feet high. Built over the shallow water of a creek where it enters the Atnarko River, the trap was closed at the upstream end while the entire downstream end was open, with a trapdoor to be dropped when the birds were lured in with grain.

· The Wildlife people left a radio-phone so they could be called whenever the swans began feeding in the trap. The birds were being fed at that time in the river where it runs through the Edwards property. My father had built a long floating bridge across the river just below the mouth of the creek where the swan trap was and I was feeding them off the bridge. As it is actually just a long raft anchored to the bank at each end, the river flowing under it speeds up and keeps the ice off. It was only during the coldest weather I packed the grain to the foot of Big Lagoon where the water stayed open due to the warm springs.

Each day I tried to entice the swans into the trap by throwing grain in. First I just put the feed in the river and up to the doorway but as they grew tamer I put all the feed inside the trap and the swans entered and ate as long as I wasn't too near. Then it turned cold. The creek and even the river froze so I had to transfer operations to Big Lagoon for a few weeks until the weather moderated and the trap area was clear of ice.

In February, 1952, when I had the swans coming into the trap again, the Wildlife people were summoned. They flew in by ski plane and a day or so later, after the swans had recovered from their fright of the landing aircraft, they were again coming into the trap to eat.

One morning I stood on a crosspole at the door of the trap and threw the grain as far up the creek as I could. Several cygnets and one or two adults swam up to the pole, clambered over it and proceeded upstream into the trap, picking up floating grain as they went. When they were well inside, I stepped across to the far end, pulled the prop out from under the gate on that side, then slowly lowered it before more than a few became alarmed and managed to slip past me. I had caught an adult and five cygnets. They panicked and tried to fly through the door but soon settled down when they found they could not. The rest of the flock outside the trap took off with a mighty roar of wings and alarmed trumpetings. There were only around one hundred of them, but even that number makes considerable racket.

Mr. Mackay, Mr. Munroe and I entered the trap slowly and as soon as the big birds found we weren't going to hurt them, they stopped trying to fly and only attempted to swim away. One of us would wade to a swan which appeared fatalistically resigned to an untimely end, gather its wings to the sides and lift it out of the shallow water. As soon as the bird felt itself restricted in this manner, it lay limply in its captor's arms. They were put into individual sacks and tied so they couldn't fight around and injure their wings. All they could move were their necks which protruded from the sacks. The cygnets were carried to my parents' house and turned loose in an 8 x 4 x 3 foot cage made of wire. They stayed there several days until shipping crates could be constructed. The cygnets were supplied with pans of water and grain. Being already used to eating grain they were soon feeding like tame barnyard fowl. In fact, they conducted themselves with a lot more dignity and good sense than most domesticated hens would!

The crates weighed close to 20 pounds each and, with a swan inside, the weight doubled. (All the swans were very thin.) Five loaded crates plus three people and gear made a formidable plane load. One crate eventually had to be left behind but whether the crateless swan sat on someone's lap or not, I don't know! I never heard how the swans liked their plane ride but at any rate they were in England two or three days later and although one died, some of the others mated and produced cygnets.

In addition to capturing the trumpeters, the Wildlife people wanted to try putting printers ink on the swans' feathers so they could be identified to ascertain migration routes and nesting areas. The marking project didn't work very well. First of all, the swans were still very nervous as a result of the recent trapping incident and secondly, they were extremely frightened by the ink which I managed to spray on one or two of them. As soon as they saw the red substance on a bird's feathers they all stampeded out of the river.

The next day none of them came into the river so I had to feed them at the north end of Big Lagoon. Even down there they kept their distance for several days. When they began to come in closer I took the chance to spray some more dye on them. Again they all fled.

Perhaps they didn't like the smell of it as it was dissolved in gasoline. Some of it fell on the water and spread toward the suspicious birds. They refused to feed in that area and as it was still too early for them to be able to feed themselves, I discontinued the marking and was forced to find a new place to feed them.

In the spring of 1953 my father built an aircraft hangar on the south end of the lagoon right across from the bridge where I fed the swans. As this structure began to grow, the swans had their real introduction to civilization with a bang—literally! The hangar was built on the ice along the shore and as it rose into the air, the swans stopped coming to the bridge entirely. They continued to come into the feeding area at the north end, nearly a mile away, although the noise of hammering and sawing must have disturbed the peace and quiet of their environment even there.

That fall the swans fed in Big Lagoon before ice came and got somewhat used to the large building. Some of the more adventurous of them even swam cautiously up the river. As nothing happened to them, more followed. When feeding time came, they once more looked for it at the bridge.

I obtained the Taylorcraft CF-HEO in the spring of 1953 and in the fall I flew several trips to Bella Coola after the swans had come in. I remember flying over the head of Lonesome Lake on my approach to land on the lagoon and being able to count fifty trumpeters under my left wing.

During the winter of 1954-55 my father did a lot of flying. The loud roar of even a small plane was something the swans were not prepared for so every time he took off the swans got scared and flew out of the area, not returning until the following day. They gradually learned to depart for the head of Lonesome Lake when the motor was started to warm up for a flight. Now, even planes as big as the DeHaviland

Beaver taking off towards them only causes them to make loud comments on the event. They rarely fly out of their feeding place unless someone makes a landing from the north and flies through the flock as it rises in front of the plane. When jets flying at great height first sped over the valley the swans worried but now they aren't even disturbed by sonic booms that nearly shatter our windows and shake the whole house.

As the winter of 1965 drew to a close, the supply of swan feed was nearly exhausted. Since the natural feeding grounds were still locked under ice, we called for more grain. This came in by helicopter just a day or two before we would have run out. They set the chopper down in front of the grain shed, one hundred feet or so from where we feed the birds, making two trips to bring in the 1,000 pounds we had requested. All the swans flew to Stillwater that day but were back the following day for their much-needed rations.

Over the years the swans have become increasingly inured to new and terrifying noises and sights. When I first started feeding them they were concerned if I so much as changed the color of my coat or if I wore a hat. Cold or rain necessitated a change in clothing and eventually they got used to it. They still protest if a person breaks the shore ice and accidentally steps into "their" water or makes a startling sound by dropping the feed dish with a clatter. I believe they are of the opinion we are land animals and as long as we stay on the shore we aren't a threat. They don't appear to mind our walking on the ice when the feed hole is frozen. On the contrary, they walk right up and look us in the eye!

For years the trumpeters wouldn't tolerate more than one person going down to the beach. If two or more people tried it, they would all start to talk in alarmed tones, then fly out until everyone had departed. As time went on and various people wanted pictures of them, they managed to get used to it. Now two or three people can go down without any display of concern by the swans.

They have never worried about a camera held in a person's hands or the click of camera shutters but they dislike a tripod being left set up on shore and won't come near it although they don't care so much if someone is with it.

Several years ago I wanted to photograph swans eating out of the grain sack, so I sat one down on the shelf of shore ice after rolling the top down to expose the food. As soon as I stepped back to take the picture they got suspicious and backed off, sounding the alarm call. Though they had previously eaten out of the sack, they lost trust in it as soon as I left it. They allowed Jack to get the picture I wanted, some years later.

Back in the late '40s the swans learned to respond to a certain call I gave just prior to feeding time. It all began quite by accident. As a kid of 12 or so, it was my chore to turn out my parents' cattle for their daily exercise and drink. At the same time the hens were turned out of their house to enjoy the sun and mess up the cow's hay in their mangers. If it was too cold, however, my mother wouldn't want them turned out. Each morning throughout the winter I would go into the barn around 11 o'clock to turn out the cows. Then I'd whoop loudly to my mother who was about one hundred feet away in the house, to ask her if she wanted the hens turned out. Soon after this loud whooping I carried the swans' breakfast down to the river for them. In time, the trumpeters came to associate my hen call with their breakfast and would come flying up, circle the fields in front of the house, give their landing call and then fly back to the river to wait!

If there was open water, I'd feed them in the river but if not I had to carry the grain to the north end of the lagoon. Many days half the flock would be at one place and half at the other. As the swans didn't know then how to pick grain off a flat, hard surface, I had to feed them in open water. I'd pack the grain down to the bridge where forty or so hungry birds awaited me, march right on across without even stopping and out onto Big Lagoon ice. One time I began calling, making a noise as much as possible like their landing call. Soon a family of swans took off from the river and flew past me down to the others. By the time I had arrived at the open water nearly all of them were there. Sometimes the river would be open but the swans continued to wait for me at the end of the lagoon. I didn't relish the idea of carrying 40 pounds of grain a mile when as far as I could see they could use their wings and fly up to the river, so I stayed where I was and called for awhile. Perhaps it was coincidence, perhaps they just got impatient. At any rate, they soon started coming in pairs and then groups. The first ones in saw the grain and called the others.

One time after I had changed locations, one of the cygnets

had an injured wing and couldn't fly, so he walked all the way up Big Lagoon, only to reach the river long after all the grain was eaten. When the flock flew back to the other end for the night, that determined and still-hungry cygnet made the mile-walk back down the ice. Since a swan takes only about six-inch steps, that poor young bird must have taken a lot of them.

The grain storage boxes were kept at the hangar until the summer of 1969 when the job had been officially transferred to us at which time we moved the boxes to a shed we built at the north end especially to house them. The government now has storage space for nearly nine tons of grain. Nine tons may sound like a lot, but when there are 400 hungry white birds clamoring for food, it is none too much. It amounts to 200 pounds a day and at that rate a box is quickly emptied. The government likes to have some kind of food reserve here so the swans won't run out before the winter ends, as has happened four times since the program started in the '30s. Twice the R.C.A.F. flew in and dropped barley on the Big Lagoon ice and one time it came in by Cessna 180 on floats and was unloaded at the hangar. The fourth time the British Columbia Game Commission brought it in by helicopter as the ice was not fit to land a ski plane on. The first time the R.C.A.F. brought the emergency supply in they used a Dakota and dropped one 100-pound sack on each run. As there were ten sacks, this required an equal number of runs. While one would think it would not be difficult to hit an area of ice nearly a mile long by a quarter-of-a-mile wide, they managed to hit just about everywhere but the ice! Three fell on the mountainside, entangling their parachutes in the trees. Two fell in the river and had to be lugged to the house for drying in the oven to forestall mould, and one exploded from the impact of hitting the ice too hard when its 'chute failed to open, scattering grain over half an acre. Another landed so near shore its parachute remained draped over the top of a tall pine tree like a great white skirt being pulled over a lady's head, while the sack lay shattered on the edge of the ice. Another job of sweeping was averted only because the sacks each had outer coverings.

We have found trumpeters are able to communicate to a certain extent. Often we find only a few birds at the feeding place when we arrive, the others being half-a-mile away.

Those at the "swannery" begin tootling and talking as soon as we get there and only a few minutes later, pairs and families fly over from the other side. Before long all of them are either circling or landing near the grain. Sometimes so many swans are in the air it is a wonder there aren't collisions but they seem adept at dodging one another. The only times they collide is when one carelessly lands so close to parked swans they must duck their heads or risk getting walloped by the huge wings.

One day after a sudden temperature drop, the feedhole was frozen over. A dozen or more swans were there awaiting their food. I watched a pair of adults come spiralling in, make a sharp turn and line up to land. They glided in fast, threw up their seven-inch webbed feet and skidded across the smooth clear ice, scattering frost crystals and parked swans in all directions! After coming to a stop, the two show-offs stood face to face, congratulating each other loudly and with satisfaction by bowing, fluttering their wings, gabbling, whooping and talking. Meanwhile, the swans that had been knocked aside so rudely simply picked themselves up, rearranged their mussed feathers, flapped their wings and sat down again.

Most winters the swans have been able to eat their grain in the water except during a few days of extremely low temperatures. Twenty below or colder usually frezes the ice so thick even the combined weight of 300 or 400 swans (amounting to perhaps 11,250 pounds) can't break it.

During the winter of '68-'69 there was a prolonged cold spell lasting about five weeks with average morning temperatures of -7°F and this caused 18 inches of ice to form. It stayed on the feeding place for weeks after the weather moderated. As there was no open water anywhere to feed the swans in, we had through necessity to spread it on the ice. The birds soon learned the technique of picking up the grains.

A swan's bill is made to shovel up mud, so the top mandible overhangs the bottom one, making it very hard for them to pick up anything small from a flat, hard surface. They were hungry, so solved the problem by turning their bills to one side and scooping the grain in, instead of trying to take it in at the tip. The grain lies in heaps when it is first thrown out onto the ice and the birds can shovel up a teaspoonful at a time, but it soon becomes more and more

31

scattered. Then they must really work to pick it up. If there is an inch or so of snow, they can shovel up the grain along with the snow quite nicely.

Too much water can make as much trouble as too much ice. I recall watching the swans feeding way up in one of the fields at my parents' place one fall. There had been a lot of rain during early November and the water rose so much they could not reach bottom in the head of the lake and Big Lagoon so they had dredged the muddy parts of the flooded fields next to the river. As this area was limited, they soon ran out of food and had to be fed starting November 20, the earliest ever.

The job normally begins in mid-December but the winter of 1969 was another extreme. That fall was so mild Lonesome Lake stayed wide open until almost Christmas and the lowest temperature had been 21°F so we didn't start feeding until January 5. There is also considerable variation in the stopping date. If the winter is relatively mild with only short sub-zero spells, the birds are apt to leave in late February, but if there is a long cold spell they are fed well into March.

When they begin to leave for their nesting grounds they do so in large numbers at first, then the more poorly fed ones disappear at the rate of a few each day. For example, when we were feeding nearly 400 the first reduction would be nearly 100. The next day almost that many more would be gone. After that, the rate would slow and even stop entirely for a few days. If it turned colder some swans would return for a few more days' feed before finally migrating. It sometimes happens that one or two swans are in such poor condition in the spring they never do migrate but remain on the lake all summer. These are generally cygnets, orphaned in the early fall, who just followed the other swans to the lake. They seem never to learn to eat grain without their parents to tell them it's all right and they subsist on whatever they can find. Some years there are groups of orphaned cygnets trying to dredge up a living on the river between our place and the Highbank Bridge, three-quarters-of-a-mile north, but they always die of starvation when the river freezes. We have tried putting wheat in the river where they work, but they ignore it and go digging up the little they can find. Even when they manage to be with the main flock at the feeding place, they just lie on the ice and refuse to follow the other swans' example.

The trumpeters arrived at Lonesome Lake late in October of 1967 and built in numbers rapidly as fall advanced. When we were forced to begin the feeding program December 13 there were close to 150. As more and more water froze, they increased until by mid-January there were 350, of which 100 were cygnets. We had been feeding only a few days when they were coming right in close and some were even reaching their long necks up to try to catch the grain out of the air. Their bills work so fast it almost creates a blur. Jack had several cygnets so tame that winter they were taking grain out of his hand.

Then things began to happen. On January 16 it rained hard and was still raining the next day. About eight inches of wet snow then fell and clung in great gobs to every branch and twig. Travelling conditions were atrocious.

By the next morning enough soggy, clinging snow had fallen to make 26 inches of the stuff in all. There was too much to walk through and it was too wet for snowshoes. Jack had to slog through it and the feeding trips which ordinarily take two hours were taking nearly double that time. The swans didn't mind, for there was plenty of open water to feed in.

Rain poured all day on the 20th but the sun shone for a few hours the next day. Around noon of the 22nd the rain began again and fell heavily and continuously the rest of the day and all night. More than two feet of snow on the hills began to melt. By the 23rd, the river had risen considerably and was the color of mud. All the small creeks that run off the mountains during periods of heavy rainfall were on the rampage.

We all went down to feed the swans that day. When we arrived we found the swans couldn't reach bottom in their regular feeding place and the only alternative was directly across the river channel from the grain shed. We launched our boat, which is stored in an adjoining shed, loaded 175 pounds of grain into it and rowed across. The swans didn't care for this procedure and panicked, flying over the head of Lonesome Lake. We threw their grain out anyway, some of it on the ice where they could see it.

Rain continued to pour out of the dark, brooding clouds and when Jack went to feed them on the 25th, the water was

33

so high he had to feed them back in what was normally dry, forested land. Since the whole area was covered with trees, logs and driftwood, the open-water feeding swans were very nervous but they were hungry enough to come in anyway.

Ice then formed on the high water and not enough swans could be bunched on one area to break it. The only place left for Jack to feed them was along the shore where the ice extended out three feet or so as the land sloped down. He fed them more than their ration since at that time they weren't very adept at picking grains up off the ice.

They were very nervous while eating in the woods and refused to climb over any driftwood. They appeared to feel trapped by the unfamiliarity of trees, seeming to realize they couldn't just spring out of the water and into the air. Lots of room is needed to flap those seven-foot wings.

Day by day the water slowly subsided. After it dropped four feet it almost stopped. By February 7 it was still a good foot above normal. The swans hadn't enough beach to get proper feeding but there was just no other place to do it.

Jack finally had to spread grain along the shore and the rest on the bodies of the densely packed swans. They ate it off one another quite calmly. With the poor feeding conditions, we thought they would stay longer than usual, but they migrated even before the water had returned to its pre-flood level.

Enthusiastic about life even on cold days, the trumpeters' exuberance boils over on days when the sun shines brightly and snow-melt is streaming from the rocks. The flock spread out on the ice, waiting to be fed, keeping up a ceaseless din. The clamor becomes more and more insistent during the delay while we count around 300 white swans and close to 100 gray cygnets. At last the census is taken and the first pan of grain is thrown out on the ice. Instantly the deafening uproar increases to a point where one's ears are assaulted as though a dozen bagpipes played at close range. As the feeding continues the swans come pushing in to the grain, shoving weaker ones aside and often engaging in feather-pulling.

One day, when the feedplace was still under ice, I watched two male swans grab each other by the wings, each one endeavouring to lift the other. They danced around this way for a minute or so, then one of them broke loose and flapped away into the flock. The victor, losing sight of his original opponent, simply grabbed the tail of the swan nearest him and was hauled all around through the section of the flock that wasn't eating. They bowled over other swans and pulled feathers! Eventually the swan who had his tail pulled, slipped loose.

Throughout the flock of 400 swans, pairs stood facing one another, wings held at half mast, bowing and trumpeting. At the conclusion of this display many more swans stood up high and flapped their great white wings, finally subsiding enough to waddle forward and resume eating. The colossal din didn't slacken off so much as a decibel during the entire performance. The sound level went down only when most of them had their bills full of grain. A comparatively soft murmur, broken by infrequent questioning trumpetings of single swans, was all that could be heard as I made my way back up the ice.

Considering the stupendous noise these birds are capable of, a very curious thing happens every once in awhile. From some signal, seemingly from just one bird, the entire flock instantly becomes mute. All heads are held erect and the swans scan their surroundings for several moments before beginning to gabble with renewed vigor.

The trumpeters were livelier, more voluble and exultant during the winter of 1969-70 than I had ever seen or heard them. Perhaps it was due to the extremely mild weather. During the latter part of January there were not just pairs of swans bowing and fluttering their wings, but entire groups. Even the cygnets were getting into the act. One day there were 10 swans, adults and cygnets, standing in a circle, heads going up and down like pistons, wings held at half mast and quivering, each one seemingly trying to outshout the others.

On another occasion one large adult male stood on the ice beside the feedhole, bent his long neck over his back in an "S" curve while holding his wings spread out stiffly. The outer portion of the wings bent down so the tips of the primaries were dragging on the ice. He slowly rotated his body, seemingly seeking another swan to attack. He did this for a minute or so, then stayed in one place, twisting his body from side to side, never uttering a sound. Finally he spied a swan gesturing in a similar manner. He walked stiffly towards it, twisting rhythmically with each slow step. When they were about six feet apart, he rushed at the other swan and they grabbed each other by their wings and pulled for a few seconds.

When they slipped loose the attacker latched onto the other's tail. Away they went, wings flailing and feet churning, around and through the other swans, knocking over any careless enough to remain standing in their path.

After proceeding wildly in this manner for 30 to 40 feet, the swan being towed let go of the other's tail and hurried back to his mate. So great was his desire to be congratulated that he half flew and half ran all the way back to her. She had been standing watching the fight throughout, shouting encouragement! They celebrated by fluttering their wings, bowing and trumpeting loudly, fairly jumping up and down with excitement and joy.

4

How the Swans Were Saved

My father, Ralph Edwards, came to public attention partly because of his pioneering adventures but mostly due to his devotion to the flock of trumpeter swans which have wintered at Stillwater and at the shallow mudflats of Big Lagoon, Lonesome Lake, for as long as human memories go back.

Lonesome Lake, the main wintering ground of these trumpeting swans, lies in a beautiful and gentle valley a few miles east of British Columbia's saw-toothed, perpetually snow-crowned Coast Mountains. It is about 280 air miles northwest of Vancouver and 50 miles inland from South Bentinck Arm, with 8,000 to 10,000-foot peaks between. Being at 52 degrees north latitude, it is only three degrees north of Vancouver and in the southern third of the province, not in "the frozen wilds of northern B.C." as it has so often been described. Lonesome is only one of 31 lakes of half a mile or more in length in the Atnarko River system. It is bigger than any of the others except Charlotte Lake to the east and it is considerably deeper than that one.

North America has two native swans, the trumpeter (*Olar buccinator*), largest of all North American waterfowl and the whistler *(Olar columbianus)*. These two species were widely distributed throughout the continent when the first white people arrived. For centuries the native Indians killed some for food and used their feathers in ceremonial wear. The

37

flocks did not suffer from such relatively minor inroads into their numbers.

In 1772 the Hudson's Bay Company was established and began buying swan skins, since there was a good price on the pure white plumage. The soft white feathers and down were used for powder puffs, quilts and feather beds while the hard, elastic quills made excellent pens.

In about 125 years the great swan flocks dwindled to such an extent there were hardly any to be had for sale. The trumpeters suffered much more than the smaller whistling swan. One reason for this was their habit of grubbing close to shore where they were easily shot from blinds while the whistlers stayed well out in the centers of lakes.

By 1838 the flocks had been so depleted they had entirely disappeared along the eastern edge of the U.S.A. and through central Canada. After nearly all the trumpeters had been killed, there sprang up in the 1900s a very lucrative trade in live birds for zoos and fancy estates both on this continent and in Europe. This may actually have helped prevent the total extermination of the species as the purveyors of live birds needed breeding stock.

The greedy and thoughtless slaughter continued past the turn of the century before people suddenly woke to the fact they had nearly eradicated the trumpeter swans. Treaties were drawn up to protect the few that were left. The U.S.A. and Great Britain signed the Migratory Bird Treaty Act in 1918, prohibiting all hunting of the beautiful birds in Canada and the U.S.A. By then there were so few of the magnificent white swans left they were considered in real danger of being eliminated. One eminent ornithologist sadly predicted in 1912 they would become extinct in a matter of only a few years as at that time there were "only a few dozen left".

Small groups of them managed to survive in hidden, inaccessible valleys. One small flock at the Red Rock Lakes area in Montana was protected and guarded well enough to make a good comeback.

In British Columbia there were several small groups clinging to life. One of these was in the Atnarko River system of which Lonesome Lake is a part. Another group was found to be wintering in the Vaseux Lakes area where a migratory bird sanctuary was established in 1922 by the Wildlife Protection Service of the National Parks Branch.

For a few years the government policy was to keep the whereabouts of any surviving groups of swans as secret as possible in an attempt to lessen the likelihood of their being molested. As the public became better educated on their plight through lectures and newspaper articles, it was agreed publicity might help the birds in their fight for survival.

The swans at Lonesome Lake were brought to the attention of the Wildlife Protection Service through the efforts of my father in the late 1920s.

In 1925 he was guiding grizzly bear hunter John P. Holman of Fairfield, Connecticut, an Audubon Society member and a man passionately fond of the wild. During conversations between guide and hunter, Holman grew intrigued by the plight of the swans and passed the story along to the Vancouver game warden.

He reported Ralph Edwards had observed "large flocks of 50 or 60 swans" up and down the lakes and rivers. The correspondence between the two friends demonstrated a continuing interest in the huge birds and it is recorded that during the winters between 1913 and 1933 ice conditions on the lakes and rivers "almost exterminated" the trumpeters. In 1926 my father reported almost 150 swans. That must have been an unusual season as Lonesome Lake stayed open nearly all winter. The Canada geese apparently remained on the lake all that season as well.

Winter of the following year was cold and many swans, particularly cygnets, starved to death as the feeding areas remained frozen for a six-week stretch. In one letter to Holman, Edwards comments: "It's too bad there could not be some way of feeding the swan during hard winters". (Quotes from "Sheep and Bear Trails" by J.P. Holman)

This suggestion started the ball rolling and in the winter of 1932-33 the Canadian Wildlife Service began to provide grain for the huge, beautiful birds whose continued existence was so threatened. My father was made officially responsible when the government made him part-time Migratory Bird Warden and paid him to keep records, protect the swans and feed them when they needed it.

Ralph Edwards horsepacked the grain in, gratis, and fed it to the birds during January when the lakes all froze up. He fed them at Stillwater which at that time was a good feeding area, having mud bottom and pond weeds in the shallow parts. Some of the grain was packed to The Birches to feed a few of the birds which stayed in the river where it flowed quietly through his land.

He dispersed 100 pounds of barley to the swans once a week, more or less. The Department suggested soaking the grain overnight in the river as they weren't sure the swans would be able to utilize the rock hard, dry grain. It didn't take the famished birds long to learn to eat the unusual food. One night they came and attacked the sack of grain where it was soaking close to shore. They worked every single grain through the loosely woven sacking and ate it without waiting for it to soak. As no harm came of this, Edwards just threw it out dry into the shallow water from then on.

He fed the swans only during the coldest spells when all natural food was locked under ice. As soon as it began to melt, the swans started digging in all available open shallow water up and down the river and lakes. They were not parasitic then and have not become so after years of feeding. They much prefer their natural food to the artificial rations.

Barley was used when the feeding program first began as it was considered most economical. However, as it was lighter than wheat, it tended to float downstream and sink in water too deep for the swans to reach it. In addition, it had a high percentage of indigestible material so I eventually suggested they try wheat. Being pure grain, heavier and of a higher protein content, wheat was not all that much more expensive in the long run. In the winter of 1974-75, the government reverted to supplying barley.

The flock gradually increased as the years went by after the feeding program was inaugurated, but in 1936 a flood dammed Tenas and Lonesome Lakes and turned Stillwater into what we refer to as Snag Lake. The natural feeding area for the birds was thus greatly reduced. With more swans and less natural food, a larger quantity of grain had to be brought in each fall.

After a few more years of increase there were too many birds to feed only once a week and since Stillwater tended to flood with every cloudburst, all the grain was brought to the Edwards' place at the south end of Lonesome Lake where the feeding took place for some years. The swans grew tamer on the daily feeding schedule and derived more benefit from the grain as they were all on hand each day and got a more regular portion. Half-a-pound a bird, daily, is a pretty slim ration for a creature weighing 30 to 35 pounds, but it seems

40

sufficient as there were few losses each winter and the flock was increasing.

Stanley and John did the feeding for some years but when they left The Birches, I was old enough to take over, which I did from the time I was 12. My father still had the job officially but since I liked the swans I was happy to take over when my father was off trapping and unavailable to do it.

The grain was horsepacked and boated in until 1948, after which it was brought in by commercial airline each year up to and including 1958. My husband and I then contracted to horsepack the grain. The first year we did this we used just two horses and packed 6,000 pounds of swan feed, plus about a ton of our own supplies. The year 1970 was the last the grain was brought in over the trail as a local airline now holds the contract. From 1959 to 1970 we moved 127,900 pounds of grain, plus nine tons of our own supplies.

There is no set amount of grain provided annually. The arrangement is that the government replaces whatever amount the swans eat each winter, plus a reserve to provide for any increase in the flock or to allow for early or late feeding necessitated by extreme weather conditions.

Where the Lonesome Lake trumpeter swans go when they migrate no one seems to have discovered, but it is obviously a good place since they raise plenty of cygnets. Even though no one has watched them nesting, there is no reason to suppose they nest differently from those under biologists' scrutiny.

An excellent source of information on nesting swans is Banke's *The Trumpeter Swan,* a complete treatise on the non-migrating trumpeters of Red Rock Lakes and a few other places. If this group behaves typically, they re-claim their old nesting sites soon after they reach the nesting lakes and set about to defend them from all other swans. Later in the spring they begin repairing the old nest or constructing a new one.

They live and feed in flocks, literally rubbing wings all winter, but as soon as they begin nesting each pair pre-empts a lake all to itself and will not allow another couple on the same lake even though it may comprise nearly 1,000 acres. A lake must cover at least nine acres or a pair won't even consider nesting on it. They prefer a shallow lake with plenty of pond weed and animal life on it.

Nest building is usually a joint effort, although the pen

41

(female) seems to do the major portion of the work. If they undertake to repair an old nest, the pen lies on top of it and hauls up material from the sides of the nest hummock, throwing it in the general direction of the nest. When she has enough aquatic growth, she arranges it to her satisfaction, completing the structure with a few feathers and bits of down as lining. The nest may be five feet high from the bottom of the lake, with about four feet of it under water.

They generally try to site their nests behind a screen of sedge or trees to conceal it from prying eyes and like to have a moat at least ten feet wide between nest and shore.

Once a nest is completed, the pen begins laying eggs. A mature bird can lay as many as ten eggs but the average clutch appears to be six. Grayish-white in color, the eggs measure 4.5 x 2.8 inches. After being brooded for about 35 days, they hatch into little white balls of down with pink bills, weighing an average of seven ounces. The cob (male) may never sit on the eggs, but he keeps constant guard throughout hatching time.

After they are hatched, both parents escort the little cygnets around in shallow water, digging up the mud to bring tiny aquatic animals to the surface. The young ones gobble greedily. They never stray from their parents, but swim and eat very close to and usually between the adult birds. For at least a month after they are hatched the mother continues to brood her babies each night.

By the time they can fly, roughly 100 days after they hatch, the cygnets weigh about 20 pounds. They seem to get flight feathers during September and October. The adult moults anytime during the summer, taking at least a month to replace flight feathers. While flightless, the swans stay on their lakes and may even resort to diving to evade an enemy.

Although they apparently mate for life, a pair broken by the death of one of them may result in the survivor seeking a new partner. At least through the second summer cygnets remain with their parents as a tight group and if scared while flightless, will not separate.

Although a nesting pair guards its lake jealously from other swans, it will frequently allow ducks and geese to share the lake. The nesting pairs remain until late summer or early fall with occasional visits and feeds with a neighbor on "neutral" water. Pairing off occurs late in the fall of the third year although they don't appear to begin breeding until the fourth or fifth year.

The job of caring for the swans was formally transferred to me in 1958 although I had actually been doing it 16 years by then. I carry on the feeding program today with the assistance of my husband Jack and daughter Susan.

The two-and-a-half-mile Trumpeter Trail is a daily winter trek which does not qualify as a leisurely stroll. Despite the fact it winds through some delightful groves of birches and evergreens and boasts a variety of vistas of mountains and river, it is an energetic jaunt.

As it is travelled daily in the winter through all kinds of weather conditions, often with the original trail-breaking having been done by the horses, it tends to develop an assortment of humps, dips and icy patches. One makes fair time as long as one remains "in step" with the trail but if the left foot lands where the right should, one can be thrown off stride.

The trail starts off across the farmyard entering the woods at the north-west corner. Usually within a short time two or three deer may be seen standing quietly and almost invisible in the dappled shadows. Tracks of squirrel, marten and fox mark the snow all along the way. Trumpeter Trail winds through trees, across small creeks and along the river bank to the south end of Lonesome Lake.

When weather conditions are right, intriguing ice formations are sculpted by the river. At one point a whirlpool is formed. When it is cold enough, ice begins to form along the river banks and a slowly revolving pan of ice forms in the center of the pool. As the shore ice widens and the pan of ice gets larger it is soon made almost circular from constantly turning on its own axis inside the shore ice.

Once on my return from a swan-feeding trip I timed the pan as it slowly gyrated. The entire revolution required five minutes. We get an excellent view of it from our trail which follows along the hillside about 30 feet above the river.

Eventually it all freezes solid and a number of circular ridges show where each layer of ice formed on the edges of the revolving pan. Seen on a clear, cold day with the sun sparkling on the huge frost crystals on the river ice and on every twig and branch along the river it is one of Nature's most impressively intricate handiworks.

Vapor rising from the open places cools and forms large

frost crystals on long streams of black moss on the undersides of every branch near the water until it resembles a strange sort of gossamer.

From the end of the trail through the woods, it is almost another mile along the ice to the "swannery". Along the edges of Big Lagoon are evidences of the playful otter with their run, slide, run, slide tracks.

Even from a distance, the trumpeting call of hungry birds can clearly be heard. Frequently a few of the gigantic swans detach themselves from the main flock and fly to greet the feeders. This may be nearly courtesy or an attempt to speed us up.

The young swans are not only noisy but very impatient. While the specified amount of grain is being taken out of the shed and brought to the shore in sacks, the swans keep up a constant nagging complaint, obviously wanting delivery of the grain as quickly as possible.

When the kernels hit the shallow water or the surface of the ice, they all mill around, eagerly scooping up the barley. All of a sudden, for no apparent reason, a wild shrieking erupts and the entire flock will scurry away, chattering nervously to themselves, huddling on the ice at a far corner of the open water. Gradually they quiet down and come back to resume eating . . .

* * * * *

5

Lonesome Lake, February 14, 1976

Lonesome Lake
February 14 (Valentine's Day) 1976

I've seen the swans! Actually, their trumpeting was my
introduction to the Turners' valley home on the day I
arrived, but I was too distracted by everything else to really
absorb the wonder of it. Each evening in winter, just prior to
sunset, flocks of varying numbers of swans leave Lonesome
Lake for unknown destinations where they spend the night.
As they fly over the Turner house, they salute it by bugling.
Since we had emerged from the woods at exactly the right
time, I had been treated to that memorable greeting.

This morning, however, is indelibly imprinted on my
mind. Three or four of those huge birds, etched chalk white
against the deep, pure blue of the sky, necks stretched and
gigantic wings spread, the sound of their warbling, fluid
bugle contrasting with the whoosh of the strong wing beats...
it all combined to form an unforgettable, moving experience.

They are fairly clumsy-looking as they waddle their way
around on the ice, but in the air they display indescribable
elegance. Everything they do is grist for the camera, from
their most ridiculous antics to awe-inspiring grace.
Trumpeters are rarely quiet, I found. In the water or on the
ice, the young cygnets in particular keep up a squawking

45

honk and of course the clear two-note trumpeting for which they are named is exceptionally beautiful.

I had seen lots of pictures of the swans before starting out on my trip and had read everything I could about those at Lonesome Lake. Nothing prepared me for the reality of seeing more than 200 of the marvellous creatures at close range.

After the energetic walk to and from the "swannery" it was always a joy to enter the warm, comfortable Turner home and to enjoy one of their memorable meals. For make no mistake, the jaunt is no reducing regime. Having slogged over the trail like a horse, one tends to come back and eat like one!

The house was originally constructed in 1958, with an addition put on in 1972 to provide more privacy for Susan and to increase storage space in the house.

The kitchen is the center of many communal activities, as in most country homes. It measures 12 x 14 feet and has three generous windows all of which provide rewarding views of the surroundings. One of these is over the sink and faces the river and hay fields, with a glimpse of snow-capped Mt. Ada. A big yellow arborite-topped table stands under the largest window which looks right up the valley. It is from this position the swans may be seen heading down toward Big Lagoon each morning, or leaving for their sleeping spots just before sundown each evening. The third and smallest window overlooks the verandah and up toward the farm buildings. The temperamental gasoline engine washing machine, brought in over the trail at huge physical expense, sits idly on the back porch.

The kitchen contains an ample supply of built-in cupboards for all supplies needed close at hand. Since various outbuildings and other storage areas are also utilized, the kitchen really only needs to accommodate a month's supply of staples and root vegetables.

The roothouse holds some of the bulk vegetables and most of the canned food. There is a frostproof underground storage room for the main stock of home-grown produce. Another building houses a vermin- and insect-proof safe for fresh meat which can hold up to 800 pounds. The same building also houses large quantities of flour, sugar and grains in a big rodent-proof box.

Although a sink is set into the kitchen counter, there is no running water in the house. The sink merely provides a handy place to dispose of water and to do such chores as vegetable-peeling, milk-straining and dish-washing.

Water is carried in, two buckets at a time, from Bear Bath Creek, about 200 feet from the house. The trail to the creek is the same one that led to "my" cabin just a little further along. It was a mystery to me why the Turners had never improved this trail which involved crossing a couple of little streams and decidedly lumpy terrain. I marvelled how Jack managed to navigate it with two full buckets, without falling on his face! Apparently it was just one of those little jobs far down on the list of priorities and he was so used to it he didn't give it a thought. At any rate, the water from the creek is deliciously sweet and clear. During the summer, a plastic pipe brings the water much closer to the house. An additional supply of water is stored in a five-gallon tank on the side of the big stove. This provides a constant supply of warm water for the frequent washups necessitated by visits to the barn or whatever.

While I was in residence, a kettle was generally kept ready for my frequent cups of coffee, a beverage the Turners consider costly and untempting. They drink either milk or water and both are outstandingly flavorful. Since I don't enjoy anything but skim milk, a special supply was put through the separator for my use and enjoyment. Dairy skim milk doesn't hold a candle to the superb beverage provided by Valerian (Sweet Mountain Flower).

The big wood stove is a four-cover type with a roomy oven and a convenient upper shelf for keeping food warm. The packing in of this incredibly heavy item is described elsewhere in the story.

On one side of the stove stands a sturdy attractive log wood box and on the other, a set of shelves to hold pots and pans. A work table is lined up beside this, under the verandah window which views the imposing supply of wood in the shed.

The opposite wall is taken up with the table where the family eats, talks, writes, reads and listens to the battery radio or stereo. Here, too, the lamp stands each evening while everyone busy at a chore in some other part of the kitchen sputters at the shadows thrown by everyone else! The lamp is lit at the latest possible hour, depending on the time of year and the weather. This is made necessary because kerosene must be conserved in order to last to the next shopping expedition and then must be packed in.

CHQM Vancouver is the radio station received most clearly although CBC can also be heard. An hour of good music is enjoyed during the course of most winter evenings and the Turners make a point of keeping up with the news. Susan listens to CHUB's Scottish music program whenever reception is good.

Opening off the kitchen is the original living room which had been enlarged by the addition to create an adjoining bed-sitting room, the combination being 14 x 22 feet in area. The wall of the room divider houses on one side the family library and on the other the collection of records together with more books and a display of rocks and shells collected by the family and augmented by contributions from friends who know of their interest.

The library includes the Audubon Nature Encyclopedia, the Standard Cyclopedia of Modern Agriculture, medical and veterinary reference books, the Time-Life Science series, a wide variety of books on horses and wildlife, including just about everything Gerald Durrell ever wrote and a good representation of works by Roderick Haig-Brown. The dictionary gets a workout in this household and is hauled out frequently to settle one question or another.

A picture-mounted cabinet beside the front door conceals the guns and ammunition, together with fishing and photographic equipment.

An Ashley heater provides additional heat to this part of the house when needed. Any sewing projects are tackled here, when Trudy and her daughter put their heads together over the treadle sewing machine to make clothes or do repairs. All such work must, of course, be done during daylight hours.

In the large sleeping section of this area is the home-made double bed beside which stands a sturdy and unique table made from the cross-section of a cedar tree supported by a root formation and braced with deer antlers. This is only one example of Trudy's innovative talents as furniture maker. A model of a sailing ship, the hull a gift to Jack, has been completed by him and stands on another table.

The record collection fills two long shelves and includes ample evidence of Susan's Scottish interests. Jack's taste runs more to Spanish melodies. In addition there are Gilbert and Sullivan albums, a good selection of classics and light classical music as well as sound tracks from shows. As a source of amusement for the entire family, there are some Dr. Seuss records, collected when Susan was younger but still played quite often on the battery stereo.

This part of the house is light and airy, boasting three windows looking both south and west. Opening off the living room is a storage room which houses most of the family's off-season clothing together with shelves laden with home-canned fruit and vegetables and other surplus kitchen supplies.

Susan's room was labelled "out of bounds" as she seemed to feel her housekeeping didn't meet the standards of tidiness evidenced elsewhere in the house! It is an 8 x 10-foot room and holds, besides her bed, much evidence of her prime interest—horses.

All the walls in the house are hung with photos of wildlife or the surrounding countryside as well as many paintings by Trudy. Her tempera and acrylics are a blend of utterly faithful reproduction and a naively idealistic interpretation of the subject. She has tried oils but did not enjoy working in this medium. Her competence and joy in her art is obvious and she clearly delights in being able to record the beauties of the land which are out of sight or season.

Her carvings and inventive use of wood also adorn the house. Window ledges and odd shelves bear potted plants. All the floors are covered with bright, shining linoleum. Ceilings and walls are of plywood in combination with chipboard. The entire effect is of cheerful, neat efficiency enhanced by attractive vistas inside and out.

Reached by an outside staircase is additional storage space in the upper loft. This contains their camping gear, spare clothing, a collection of heterogenous pieces of metal for use in improvising machinery repairs, outsize cooking pots such as that used for canning, snowshoes, garden gunny sacks and spare jars, boxes and Christmas decorations.

Considering the comfort and convenience of the house, even though it lacks what are considered necessities by city folk—running water, electricity and inside plumbing—and adding to this the high standard of living evidenced by their excellent diet, it is incredible to discover how modest their actual cash requirements are.

I asked Jack to average out his income over the past 18

years and the result was unbelievable. The average income has been $1,700, with the high being $2,500 and the low $900. This covers the period 1957-1975 and includes income from their swan-feeding job, writing, sale of beef and miscellaneous investments.

One element, rarely seen but constantly felt in the Turner household, costs no money at all. The home is furnished with love. Perhaps, this being Valentine's Day, I was particularly tuned in to it!

Trudy tends to say little about those things in her life which mean the most to her. For example, her own account of meeting and marrying Jack Turner is handled very tersely in the course of describing the development of Fogswamp. "Then in January, 1957, Jack Turner and I were married in Bella Coola. After that, progress was much faster."

She makes only brief mention of their courtship in her journal. "Jack was born in Vancouver but grew up both here and on the south coast. Exploring the province for a place to live, he made a trip through our valley. We got acquainted while hauling trees off a new clearing I had made over the winter. He was just here for a few days but came back to the area the next summer. Then he went back outside for four months to earn a little more money before finally marrying and settling down here."

Jack, however, is far more articulate on the subject and Trudy's true feelings can best be gauged by watching her eyes light up as Jack describes how they came to be man and wife.

Jack starts out by explaining how he came to feel as he does about civilization versus wilderness. His teen years were profoundly influenced by the insecurity of the depression. He made up his mind very early that he would never allow himself to be in the position of having to be dependent on someone paying him a salary to provide for his food and a roof over his head. He knew from first-hand experience this was a precarious way to live, particularly in hard times. He vowed he would establish himself in a manner that would make him somewhat immune to the vagaries of the country's economy and in a position where he would have only himself to depend on.

"I wanted a place of my own. I didn't want it in a city, or even in a village for that matter. I wanted more than a quarter of a mile between houses. I preferred quite a few miles, because that is my nature."

50

Jack had spent about ten years working around various parts of British Columbia in the course of his employment as a timber cruiser and assistant in laying out roads for a number of logging companies based in the Vancouver area. His travels gave him the opportunity he wanted, to search for his own piece of land. He explored many wilderness regions, always keeping in mind his prerequisites for a homesite.

In May, 1953, during his two weeks off work, Jack first came to the Bella Coola valley region. He approached it from the direction of Williams Lake, travelling into Anahim Lake, then following a trail to the first habitation he came to. The man who lived there, a long-time resident of the district, was lonely and welcomed a spot of company. He invited Jack to spend a few days. During this time he regaled his visitor with stories of the valley and of the Edwards who lived 22 miles south-east of him, fairly close neighbors by local standards.

"It was just country gossip," explains Jack, "but I was interested in all I could learn about the area, so I listened." What he learned most about was the Edwards' young daughter. She was described in glowing terms. Jack was told of her initiative, her survival abilities, capabilities, total lack of artifice and her attractiveness. He also learned there wouldn't be any point in going on to meet the family at that time since Trudy was then in Vancouver getting her pilot's license.

Jack filed the information away although at that time he was more interested in living close to the sea than locating an inland place to live. Having grown up on the coast, he had it in his mind to get a fishing boat which, together with a land base where he could grow his own food, would make him almost totally self-sufficient.

"However, I was somewhat taken with the description of the daughter and if I'd had the time then, I'd have gone to see her. But anyway, she'd already gone to Vancouver," Jack recalled.

He couldn't make it back the following year because of certain family obligations and business commitments. Still, the thought of the wilderness-wise young woman stayed in his mind. So it was that in 1955 he used his time off to come and explore the Bella Coola valley a little more, "but mainly to see the Edwards' daughter."

Which is how it happened that as Trudy was going about

her chores as usual one April day, a tall, blond man came free-striding out of the woods and into her life!

He spent just five days at the farm at that time, helping the family with their work and earning approval by his energy, his knowledgeable way with an axe and general attitude toward life. Through some strange coincidence it always seemed his helpfulness centered on whatever Trudy happened to be working at. When his brief visit was coming to a close, he told Trudy he would like to come back

Trudy now says she accepted this statement of his with a certain degree of cynicism. She refused to absolutely believe or set her heart on it because, in her words: "If you want something to happen, you shouldn't pay too much attention to it. You know, if it has been stormy for a long time and the sky appears to brighten, you don't say anything about it. If you do, it might cloud over again."

Nevertheless, true to his word, Jack returned the following year. He clearly remembers the date on which he arrived. From June 9 to September 1, Jack and Trudy worked side by side at whatever needed doing, spending a good deal of their time at Trudy's own homesite.

"After about a month, I could see that there was a good chance I would be staying on here in the future," Jack continued, in a low, quiet voice. Expanding on that concise statement, Jack explained that although they had not made any formal commitment, he and Trudy had begun to feel "there was a good chance we would accept one another." Apparently they reached this conclusion mutually and agreed they wanted the same kind of life and were prepared to work hard to achieve it. At that point, they set a date.

There had been some discussion about Jack's own desire to be near the sea, but he quickly realized that Trudy had already put in a lot of work on her pre-emption and in addition, had a huge emotional investment in the trumpeter swans. He felt he couldn't offer anything to compete with the life she had made such a good start on, so they agreed to continue at Fogswamp.

Trudy's engagement ring cuts down trees! As jewellery is not too practical for the sort of adventure they were about to embark on, they decided that in lieu of a ring on her finger, Jack would leave her with the power saw as his pledge, while he went outside to collect some more money.

Jack spent a final Christmas with his own parents on Salt-spring Island before returning to Lonesome Lake on December 27, 1956.

The two of them planned to fly out to Bella Coola for the brief ceremony and they took off for there in the plane jointly owned by Trudy and her father. Half-way to Bella Coola they were turned back by a blinding snowstorm. They then set out on foot, stopping on the way at a trapper's cabin owned by distant relatives of the Edwards. Finally they arrived in town where they were married in the preacher's home.

Such a romance between two young people is very touching, but one that has grown and matured for twenty years is far more remarkable and moving.

Today, Trudy, at five foot three and a half, is a compactly attractive woman, her gray hair cut very short around her fine-featured face. Her most striking aspects are her eyes, bright blue and lively. Her forehead is high and her slightly prominent nose is perhaps all that keeps her from conventional beauty.

Jack is five foot eleven and a half inches tall. His light brown hair has vanished from the top of his head to some extent, but the loss is compensated for by a crop of black chin whiskers! He has a straight nose, deep-set clear hazel eyes and a ready-smiling wide mouth.

As a couple who celebrated their twentieth wedding anniversary January 9, 1977, they present a picture of energetic companionship, enjoying life to the brim.

It takes a watchful eye to catch any sign of sentiment between Jack and Trudy. At the same time, they constantly extend supportive affection to one another. Little courtesies say more than words. There is an obvious willingness to cooperate and to adapt to one another's wishes and plans with good humor.

Life is not a serious business at Fogswamp. There is a constant stream of playful banter and teasing going on between all three members of the Turner clan who obviously enjoy a bit of horseplay whether it is throwing snowballs or chasing one another around.

The relationship between Jack and Trudy appears to an outsider to be one of deep and trusting friendship, utter commitment to each other and the life they share, an enjoyment of work, play and each other, together with pride in and love for their daughter Susan, who was born February 19, 1959.

According to Trudy, progress at Fogswamp Farm was a little short of "full steam ahead" during the fall of 1958 and the spring of the following year. The explanation for this was the arrival of a 6½-pound baby daughter who was christened Susan B. Turner. There's no middle name—that choice is left to her when and if she wants to make it.

The birth took place in Vancouver, the Turners having left their isolation the first of January to stay in a rooming house in the city until time to enter the hospital. During her pregnancy, Trudy visited a doctor in Bella Coola only a couple of times. Her outstandingly good health helped her through the lengthy delivery caused by the fact that Susan made her debut in the breech position. When asked if she had breast-fed her daughter, Trudy, who believes in following the most natural path at all times, all but snapped, "Of course!"

The Edwards looked after the Turner's stock during the period they were away but when they returned March 16, chores began where they had left off. With a baby to care for, they were unable to do as much outside work as they had managed previously. According to their account of the situation, Jack spent a good deal of his time in the house and certainly did his share of changing the young baby and washing diapers. The latter, incidentally, were often scrubbed in the icy cold waters of the Atnarko River.

Jack explains the reason he took over house chores was simply that it made sense. The barn had always been Trudy's sphere. Having been brought up with animals from her earliest years, she is the acknowledged expert. Therefore it seemed logical to this efficiency-minded family that she keep on with this job while Jack kept the home fires burning, literally and figuratively.

Trudy claims she's married to one of the first truly liberated men and figures she probably invented women's lib, simply by living it! There's no crusade involved, however; it is just a matter of each doing what makes the most sense at the time.

Jack and Trudy have been devoted parents from the very start. Blending common sense with a high degree of sensitivity, they have made an outstanding job of rearing a well-adjusted, self-confident daughter. Susan, despite the isolation of her formative years, shows every indication of being capable of handling herself in a wide range of situations.

At one point in her childhood, Susan was pathetically shy and terribly afraid of meeting strangers. Once Trudy and Jack became aware of this, they made every effort to create more opportunities for Susan to be exposed to people by increasing their mail trips and taking extra journeys to Vancouver.

Taking in a foster child or two as companions for their little girl was considered but when two children from down the valley came in to spend a summer, the Turners felt the dissension it created was not helping the situation. For one thing, Susan had been alone for so long by then it wasn't easy for her to share her situation. In addition, according to Susan, she and one of the other little girls just "didn't hit it off at all."

"Susan spent a lot of her spare time reading, riding horses and calves and throwing snowballs at her parents. At eleven years of age she could milk a cow as well as I. She was nearly as tall as I but I could still push her down in the snow to repay her for throwing snowballs down my neck when my back was turned. Horses were her favorite animals," says Trudy of her daughter as a pre-teener.

There was one brief try at having a dog but Susan admits she lacked the patience and perseverance necessary to train a dog properly and ended up with a pet that wouldn't do anything she wanted it to. The dog now makes its home with Susan's grandmother at The Birches, where it continues to be spoiled, loved and untrained!

Following in her mother's steps, Susan's schooling has been basically through correspondence enriched by family discussions and free access to the extensive library the house contains.

"Susan began her education in 1965, through correspondence courses provided by the British Columbia government," Trudy explained. "We teach her the required work and then send the completed papers to Victoria where teachers correct the work and return it to us. This service is paid for by taxes for the most part and we have to buy only a few items.

"The first two years went quite smoothly as the school people hadn't made us teach 'new math' but since then the arithmetic has been confusing both to me and my student. Some of those methods must have been thought up by someone who was trying his level best to make the subject as difficult as possible. However, we gradually conquered each new obfuscating example.''

During her school years, from which she is currently taking a holiday after completing Grade 8, Susan reports she liked spelling, hated Math and didn't mind French. During my visit I discovered both Susan and her mother delight in trying out French phrases. These are probably grammatically correct, but since all their learning has been through books, their pronunciation tends to be slightly unorthodox, to say the least! Jack refuses to have anything to do with their efforts in another language!

When asked about the relative advantages and disadvantages of growing up as she did, Susan responded in her typically methodical way, by drawing up two lists. She feels she probably had a better overall diet than the average city youngster would have and that she was fortunate in avoiding early exposure to drugs, smoking and drinking.

Her reaction to education by correspondence was dual. There was the advantage of being able to work at one's own pace and to alter the year's work to fit circumstances. On the other hand, it was impossible to carry on a question-answer dialogue. It always took a long time to get replies to problems and a student tends to take longer than necessary to complete a grade.

Although her life provided early opportunities to assume personal responsibility, Susan deeply missed association with peers and contact with other people of any age, when she was young.

Susan, who celebrated her 17th birthday during my visit, says she has never felt any sense of inferiority in being a girl. As a matter of fact, both her parents have preached against it for all her life, and their own life style underscores their beliefs.

She feels willing to tackle just about anything she might have a chance to try. On the other hand, like so many of her age, she feels she has no real goals at the moment. She cannot decide what it is she would like to do, although she does not plan to stay at Fogswamp forever. She may well end up in a similar sort of situation, though, for Susan has no love of city lights. She, like her mother before her, has a hankering for a place of her own, one day.

In recent years, Susan has been out of Lonesome Lake a number of times without her parents. In 1974 she got her first paying job. In April she flew out to Bella Coola with the local airline and began working at the lodge in Tweedsmuir Park, for the people who bring the Turners' mail in from the town. The following year she worked at the same place, then spent several weeks travelling around the province with some students who were conducting an animal study in connection with provincial parks. She made trips around the Burns Lake, Smithers and Prince George regions as well as to Mt. Robson Park, Vancouver and Victoria. During this excursion her parents, who had been visiting Jack's mother on Vancouver Island, joined up with their daughter in Nanaimo.

The summer of 1976 saw Susan employed as a trail ride assistant (wrangler) at a Watch Lake dude ranch near 100 Mile House.

Christmases are bigger events in the Turner household than they were in Trudy's childhood. Jack brought a great selection of ornaments for the Christmas tree from his own home. These evoke good memories for him and he feels strongly the importance of his daughter having the same sort of traditions during her young years to assure happy recollections for her to carry into the future.

Cutting the Christmas tree is a very important business with the Turner trio seriously debating the comparative merits of the hundreds of trees surrounding their farm, before making their choice. They tend to put the tree up rather early and keep it up until after Jack and Trudy celebrate their wedding anniversary.

Anyone going through Susan's photograph album would be impressed by the number and quality of photos recording her growing years. The pictorial chronicle covers every important event in her life from babyhood through her childhood to the present. There are snaps of Susan on a succession of horses, pictures of her sitting on a cow's back or being carried on the back of one parent or another. She is shown enjoying a joyous Christmas or blowing out the candles on a birthday cake. There are very few photos of Susan in a dress and even those few indicate she felt she was taking part in a charade!

For her 1961 Christmas she received a wooden horse carved by her mother. This was mounted on runners so she could be pulled around on it. It was brought in again for Christmas three years later, at which time the horse had been provided with a miniature pack saddle.

These days Susan competently fits a real horse with a utilitarian pack saddle and accompanies her parents on the long treks in and out of the valley on the big supply-hauling pack trips.

Susan is quite clearly devoted to both of her parents, although she is currently into a period of growing independence. She is a solidly built girl, five-foot-four in height, with greenish-hazel eyes, long medium brown hair and a face of composure and gentle beauty.

The relationship between the Turners and the Edwards is one which works to the advantage of all but it has not been particularly close since Trudy set up on her own. Jack has a great deal of respect and a certain amount of admiration for Trudy's father but the two men were never very fond of each other. There may have been a degree of resentment on the part of the senior man who felt Jack benefited both from the work already done and through the advances of mechanization. All this made life a few degrees easier for Jack than it had been for Ralph Edwards when he first made his way into the valley. There could also have been some jealousy aroused when Jack walked off with the capable young woman who had worked by his side for so many years.

Today there is relatively little visiting back and forth between the two families although both Trudy and Susan give Mrs. Edwards a hand when it is asked for. However it has been worked out, the residents of Lonesome Lake seem to have discovered the secret of harmonious living. Fogswamp is a happy place and the way in which it developed is described by Trudy . . .

6

Establishing Fogswamp Farm

During the winter of 1957 Jack and I cut trees for all the logs required for a house. These had to be peeled while the bark adhered tightly to them, a slow but necessary process, to leave the coming summer clear for haying, gardening and building. We were also helping my parents on a work-machinery-sharing basis. During most of the winter one of us spent about three hours each day making the five-mile round trip to feed the trumpeter swans.

In March we left our two horses, Thuja and Rommy, plus four cattle, at my parents' place (we had hay credits there) and flew to Vancouver in the Taylorcraft seaplane. Jack wanted a flying licence so he too could fly the T-craft.

During the time we were in the city we located and purchased a wood range. This was shipped to Bella Coola and eventually trucked to Atnarko. At the end of April we took the horses down to Atnarko to get the stove. As we didn't have either rafts or boats at that time I walked the horses around the lakes while Jack took the packing gear down the lakes in borrowed boats. The entire stove weighed around 400 pounds so had to be considerably dismantled before it could be packed on the horses. All small parts were removed but that still left the main oven section and stove top. This we turned upside-down over Thuja's back, resting it on boxes of nails on each side to keep the heavy stove from turning the saddle on her back. The whole works was roped on by a special hitch. Thuja had more than 260 pounds on her back but she carried the odd, top-heavy load carefully and well.

The house was completed enough to move into on December 4. We were lucky to have mild weather and over that first winter made our own sashes and installed the large windows as fast as possible. Since the floor and ceiling were just split cedar planks, they were not very warm so we nailed dried cow hides all over the floor and as much of the ceiling as we had hides for, fur side out. These were from Ayrshire cattle, and quite picturesque. That is about all the good that can be said of them, except they did serve the purpose of keeping the cold out to some extent. Time was to demonstrate that hairy cow hides are the most atrocious kind of ceiling paneling anyone could dream up! They collected dust, moths, dirt and bugs. In short, they were a ghastly mess. The hair fell down on whatever was below. The moths ate themselves out of cow hair and since there were a great many of them, they then gobbled up everything in the house. As if the dust and dirt weren't enough to have fall onto one's eyes at night, the tiny grains of sand-like material that is moth excreta dropped regularly on every square yard of floor bed or table.

Moths didn't live in the hides on the floor but all the dirt tracked in from outside sifted to the bottom and dried to a fine dust which couldn't be swept out although it came out of the hair readily enough whenever anyone walked across the floor. Then it would ascend in a sort of haze, to the ceiling. After awhile it got heavy enough to fall back down to the floor, starting the whole joyous round again! The hides made a soft, quiet floor covering that was extremely durable and were not so bad when the hair was removed but, oh, the dust! (The hides are gone now, replaced with more conventional but easily cleaned plywood and linoleum, brought in on Jack's back over the trail.)

Another way in which we use cowhide is as dog food. I cook the scraps and sometimes whole hides for this purpose. Cut in three-or four-inch squares, and boiled four hours, it becomes tender and when it cools, a thick jelly forms on it. The dog likes this and enjoys it mixed with commercial dog food, some fat and cooked potato added occasionally.

Rawhide is also used in place of leather to a certain extent. It must be worked over a corner of metal in order to soften it

60

up, a process which must be done while the material is damp, and continued until it is dry. The rawhide can be made fairly soft in this way but must be reworked if it gets wet. Rawhide is stronger than leather so we use it for the rigging on our packsaddles and some parts of the home-made harnesses. Hames straps are all right made of rawhide. The traces are 3/8 inch steel cable spliced onto commercial steel hames and, of course, the collars are purchased. The remainder of the straps and lines are of rawhide. Complete harnesses are very expensive and we have lots of free cowhide. The material can be improved by soaking in a solution of salt, alum and water for a week or so, but still must be worked a lot to make it soft enough for use.

We also build our own packsaddles. Each one is designed to fit the horse since no two horses have identical backs. We have found this has saved a lot of trouble with sore backs, an important factor when we must depend on them for carrying heavy loads over many rough miles. I built my own riding saddle too and covered that with rawhide. We don't actually ride horses any vast mileage here as there is too much brush and rough trail. We use horses to cross rivers when necessary. I enjoy riding but prefer to be able to *go* somewhere... at a gallop, by choice!

All the very heavy work is done by horses. When we built our woodshed in 1958 we had no road to a stand of good cedar which was located at the south-west corner of the place. The horses packed the shakes in on their backs. We tied them in bundles of 80 or 90 pounds and put one on each side of the horse, with more on top. We have since made a road to the area so we can now use a wagon.

The woodshed is 15 x 22 feet and holds a year's supply of unpiled, unsplit wood. As we have an Ashley heater we get by with much less wood than with an Airtight heater. The Ashley can be filled with big logs at bedtime and will burn quietly all night with no attention. It has a thermostat which is set for the desired heat.

An underground pit was constructed for vegetable storage, but the first fall we used it we discovered we had built it right in the center of an underground spring! There was a lot of rain which caused the creeks to rise and the spring came up, flooding the potatoes and carrots, necessitating the removal of all vegetables to the house to dry. We then put in a raised floor about a foot above the bottom of the pit to keep the vegetables above water.

The following year we built a 12 x 8 foot roothouse partly above ground. The outside wall is cedar logs about a foot through. There is another thinner cedar wall and the space between them is filled with fir punk to a depth of about two feet around the walls and three feet over the top. A shake roof keeps the rain off. The double insulated door is large enough to walk through carrying a sack of spuds. This roothouse, even with all that insulation, can't keep out more than 44 degrees of frost. Some freezing occurs whenever it gets colder than 5°F. It has not got cold enough in the roothouse to break glass jars yet, though when it went to -34° F in 1968, tin-lidded jars froze and the contents expanded enough to push the lids off. We keep these in the house now as well as any jars containing very liquid material like tomatoes. We have almost ceased storing potatoes and carrots in the roothouse as they are ruined if they freeze.

One winter a pile of carrots about three feet thick froze to the center while the potatoes froze down a foot from the top. Fortunately we had lots of them so we still had enough to eat. The frozen vegetables were fed to the stock before they had time to turn black and become rotten or spoiled. Potatoes that have been frozen and thawed turn black and become very poisonous, unfit for anything.

Land clearing has gone on for years. At first we cut down all the trees on areas we hoped to make into fields. We then burned everything except such poles and logs as we could use for fences, building or fuel. We used a borrowed horse-powered winch with 200 feet of cable to pull out stumps. Most of the stumps were around 10 inches but our arrangement allowed us to pull stumps up to 30 inches in diameter. The largest ones had to have a lot of their roots cut before the machine could extract them and turn them over. After the dirt and part of the roots had been removed from the stump it was taken to the river where it was arranged to form a solid wall five feet wide and eight feet high along the soft soil of the vertical river bank. This was our project to stop erosion by the river.

In the spring of 1967 a lot of huge rocks were piled on top of these stumps. Even so, the flood of 1968 washed the whole thing out and we had to start all over again.

Our next effort was to try tying whole trees to the bank

with cable. We bought 550 feet of 3/8 inch steel cable and about 80 cable clamps. In the spring we fastened entire trees to cedar stakes driven four feet into the ground. These had been hauled from across the river to form the breakwater.

As the water is too cold and deep for wading, I rode Thuja and guided Rocket in the work of hauling the trees across. Where trees on the bank were growing far apart, allowing room to haul the trunks close enough, we simply rolled them in on top of those already forming the bank and cabled the breakwater trees to the living clumps of alders. After putting in a layer or two of trees, we hauled large rocks and dumped them on top of the branches. We then added more trees, followed by more rocks, creating a sort of hero tree-rock sandwich!

A great chunk of granite weighing close to a ton was hauled to the breakwater. To unload it we took the team across the river and drove them onto a sandy bar directly across from where the stoneboat with the rock on it was parked. A chain sling was fixed on the rock and connected to a 7/8 inch rope fastened to the team's doubletrees and I drove the team forward about a horse-length. The large, flat chunk flopped over onto the trees, sinking them well down against the eroding river bank.

We used that heavy rope many times, putting trees in place on various sections but finally had to choose between it and our two mares!

We wanted to bring a spruce across the river and tie it against the bank on the field side but the current prevented the horses from hauling it to where it could be swung across to the opposite bank at the right place. I tried driving the horses farther into the water to enable the tree top to float, but the horses in the deeper water became less able to pull. So we left the tree beached and drove the horses across to the field. Fastening the rope to the tree, we again tried to get the horses to pull it up-river to the desired position. The river makes almost a right-angle bend at this point so we had the rope stretched across the corner from the bar to the team in the field. A clump of precious alders growing on the edge of the bank prevented us from pulling at a more upstream angle. Just as the straining mares hauled the tree clear of the beach, the current caught it and started dragging the team slowly but inexorably toward the six-foot-high cut bank. When they felt themselves being pulled backwards with such force, they both gave up and tried only half-heartedly to move forward again.

They obviously weren't going to save themselves and something had to be done quickly or the two black mares would have gone backwards over the embankment into five feet of water. I shouted to Jack to chop the rope. He happened to be near an axe so he grabbed it and rushed to where the taut rope was slowly sliding along the alder clump, stripping off the bark as it moved. He severed the rope just 20 inches from the steel clevis on the doubletrees. At the rate the rope was moving, that short distance would have been used up in seconds. Jack followed the tree downstream and retrieved the cut rope. We lost the tree, however. It was swept on down the river and later on, when the water rose, it came to rest against the head of an island.

Whenever possible we leave trees and bushes along the banks, even planting some in an effort to prevent erosion. There still remain four stretches in the half-mile section of river where we have trouble. The battle to contain the river and not lose any of our precious hay fields continues to this day.

Our horses at that time, Thuja and Rommy, did most of the stump-hauling in an old stoneboat, a vehicle which is actually a strong sled with a low deck. It is constructed of naturally bent birch logs, hewn down to a good sled runner shape. A piece of fir, four feet long, is pegged to the front ends of the runners with two-inch maple pegs. The back ends of the runners are held together in the same manner. The deck is made of split cedar planks, nailed on with six-inch spikes. The horses pull on a chain which goes through a hole in the front crosspiece, up over the stumps and around the rear crosspiece. In this way, tension on the chain holds the stumps. Some of the stumps were so large we had to use the team just to load them on the stoneboat.

The spring after we got Rocket we were hauling the final batch of pulled, cleaned stumps when Rommy made it very clear he had no intention of spending the rest of his life working so hard. He wouldn't do his share of the work and as Thuja couldn't haul the load alone, we rolled it off the sled and left it.

One big stump would still be there if we hadn't decided to try the relatively "green" Rocket. We hadn't considered her a draft horse since she is about 200 pounds lighter than either

64

Fogswamp—the hand-hewed log buildings built by Trudy and Jack Turner.

Winter confinement. In periods of heavy snow, outside activities are limited to feeding the livestock and cutting down small trees for deer and moose to feed on.

Coast mountain offers beautiful alpine lakes and meadows just a few feet directly above Fogswamp's Atnarko Valley home. A few days set aside for an annual holiday in the open meadows is a much looked forward to treat.

The majestic Trumpeter Swan was brought back from near extinction early in the century to a flourishing population level today. Many conservationists feel that a major turning point in the birds' survival was the supplemented feeding program initiated by Ralph Edwards and carried on by his daughter Trudy and her husband and daughter. Eight to twelve thousand pounds of grain are fed annually.

Each swan gets a half pound of grain per day but only during the harsh weather when natural foods are very limited or unavailable. Only after several years of feeding did the huge 35-50 pound birds become tame enough to eat from hand.

Juvenile Trumpeter Swans have the gray plumage—the adults are pure white. The brownish tinge to the white heads is due to mineral stains from the water.

Thuja or Rommy. We discovered the plucky little Rocket has only one idea when hitched to a heavy object and that is to pull with every ounce of muscle in her compact body. We didn't know this until we tried her on the big stump but as we didn't want it to remain in the middle of the field, we agreed to give her a try.

Rocket and Thuja were hitched to the stump. They pulled it up until it overbalanced onto the stoneboat. We then hitched both horses to the sled. After two or three false starts to get the feel of working together, the pair took off, using both hind feet in the kind of jumping, lunging motion which provides a horse with its maximum power output. They took it the necessary 200 feet without stopping. When they came to a halt, their sides were heaving with the tremendous effort.

Rocket continues to be an almost fanatical puller, yet at the same time will haul the mowing machine as if quite conscious that hitting the cutter bar on a stump would break it and is always ready to stop if it hits anything solid. She hauls the wagon carefully, too, and if it begins to sink in soft mud, will lunge to lift it out.

We have found our geldings to be much lazier than the mares, preferring to take life easy when hard work comes their way.

Over the years we have built a lot of fencing to keep deer out of the hay fields and garden and to contain stock. It is seven feet in height and the horizontal poles are about eight inches apart. Some of it is snake fence made of 6 to 12-inch poles while the rest consists of rails nailed to posts set in the ground. The main deer fence around the place is more than one mile long.

The narrow strip of land we farm is only about 100 feet wide at each end. There are about 20 acres of arable land on the west side of the river. The east side is covered with big Douglas fir timber, rocks and steep mountain side. The river divides into several channels with two major islands formed of good land which we use for pasture. We don't dare clear them of all trees and stumps for fear they will wash away and have fenced only one of them so far.

The fences are intended to stop deer but they are not too effective in this. Nor do they always stop bear or foxes. Grizzlies, the main bear here, climb over the snake fence and slide through the rail fences. They come in any time we are gone but have done no great damage yet, except when a sow and her two cubs came into the garden the first year we were raising one here, tearing out squash and potatoes. It was mid-day and we were making a racket working on the new house just 200 feet away. That group got into rather serious trouble when we discovered what they were up to and we've not been bothered since!

The only other creature to get into mischief in the garden was a fox which persisted in digging out young asparagus plants and leaving them on top of the ground. He didn't eat them and we never actually saw him, but his tracks were in the holes he dug. I tied the dog in the garden to see if she would frighten the fox off but judging by the tracks the next morning, they must have had a nice friendly chat instead.

We have given names to our boats and rafts, and our gates as well have been christened. The one in the main outside fence bears the title Friendship Gate. If someone wishes to get to the house during the time the hay crop is growing, the visitor must follow the snake fence to Early Gate. Milk Gate might still stand closed in their path. The trail passes through this gate and continues along to Acamar Gate, hinged to a tall cedar stump and latched by a chain and slide pole to a post that supports the fence. By following an obvious trail over the ridge, past the abattoir and roothouse, past the bull pen, on beyond the henhouse and barn, one arrives at the house, set out in the middle of a field of lush grass and surrounded by a low white picket fence with shrubbery and bushes inside.

We can be by-passed quite easily and there is never any need to climb over our fences at all. One year a couple of people came to see us and for reasons best known to themselves, squirreled over the seven-foot fence. Once over, they wallowed right through some of our best hay crop to get to the house. The resulting trail resembled one made by an obese grizzly.

Even our fields have received appellations. There is Lizzy Meadow which lies next to the river, the Garden, and Gibraltar field with its distinctive eight-foot granite boulder sticking up out of the black soil. In front of the barn is the Desert, a field that contrasted strongly to the heavily timbered surroundings when we first began clearing.

On the east side of the house and on a lower level is Swamp Field. Beyond this is Oat Field, bordered on one side by the river where our longest breakwater protects it from erosion. Upi Crossing leads to September Island, the largest of the seven in the river. Then there's Beaver Pond field and Apple Bridge, where ducks and sometimes the odd hungry orphan cygnet eat in the muddy bottom of the beaver pond. There's even Bottle Tree, a large cedar shaped like a bottle at the butt and only about 60 feet tall although seven or eight feet in diameter at its grotesquely swelled base.

All the island have names, too. In addition to September, and Pup Island where I felled the tree on my dog, there are Round, Gooseberry, Slim and October Islands. On the east side of the river lies Kokanee and a little farther downstream east of Bear Island is Lynx-cat Island. Bear is the only one we have partially cleared, seeded and fenced and is situated about 100 feet north of the house. To get onto it we have a drawbridge to keep animals from walking down the river and escaping from the island. Sections of fence hang from the bridge and can be raised or lowered, depending on whether we wish to keep stock on the island. At the river end of Blackjack Bridge, is Lucky Gate, originally built to keep our horse Lucky on Bear Island one winter.

Topsy Knoll is a spot on the east side of the river up the steep mountainside. It recalls where one of my parents' horses used to run and hide whenever she heard an airplane and could get out of the pasture to escape it. If that horse was foraging anywhere within five miles of the knoll she'd run to it for protection from the plane.

Gradually over the years, our small world has evolved. Building the house was an ongoing affair for many seasons. Increasing the fields under cultivation continues and of course simply maintaining the whole area takes a great deal of time, planning and effort.

Jack and I were able to find time in 1959 to build a Douglas fir raft which had a carrying capacity of 2,700 pounds. We had the grain transporting job at that time as well as that of feeding the birds and before long we realized something with a much better payload would be required. We had a 10 h.p. Mercury outboard and decided to build a 36-foot cedar raft. During the winter of 1960 we procured logs for it. The new raft, being of cedar, would be much more buoyant and thus capable of carrying heavier loads.

We cut six logs 36 feet long and two feet at the butt and hauled them to a place along the river where they could be rolled into the river during flood. The raft was constructed by placing a piece of 3/8 inch steel cable around all the logs a few feet from the front end, tightening it with a load binder, then putting on a piece of heavy chain in place of the load binder so it could be used again to fasten the cable to the stern of the raft. A deck made of heavy planks, four inches thick, laid crosswise, created a solid platform to pile freight on or for animals to stand on.

We ran the raft down-river to the Edwards' floating bridge and to get past this obstacle, and to dismantle it, and haul it out one log at a time ready to be rolled back into the river for reassembly.

After loading a bunch of shakes we had hauled down from our place for the grain shed roof, we drove the raft to the north end of Big Lagoon. There we assembled a corral with tie rail on the raft so four animals could stand side by side. Later we added room for a fifth animal. This high floating raft we named the TX Balsa. TX stands for Trumpeter Express, the name we gave ourselves as a transportation outfit.

During Susan's baby years we also built a dugout canoe to use for a boat until we could make a proper one. It held us all well enough but we were restricted to using it only on calm days as the bow wasn't very high and spray would come in over the top.

A stable and barn combination was the last big construction job. This is 30 x 48 and 30 feet high at the ridge. The ground floor area is half hay section, 30 x 24, and the peak is over this. The other half of the ground floor is a log stable which also measures 30 x 24 feet. The stable section is immediately below the hay, making feeding no problem. The hay is just pitched into the mangers for the animals. The stable has stancheon room for two cows, two calves, one bull in a box stall, a 10 x 10 stall for cows to calve in, plus stall room for four horses tied up with halters.

The hay section is large enough to hold 16 tons of hay, with more room over the stable ceiling for surplus hay. The ceiling is composed of a set of poles covered with hay during the winter. The hay is removed each spring and new hay dried on those and other rack poles in the main hay section. Hay can in this way be cured in the barn when there is too much rain to dry it in the field.

We rake the grass up wet, haul it in small bundles in the

wagon and with a rope and pulley system the team shift the bundles one at a time from the wagon to the loft. One of us drives the horses while the other is up on the racks in the top of the barn with a special landing rack. The team lifts the bundle of heavy, often dripping grass to the block in the top of the barn and holds it there while the landing rack is slid under. The horses are backed, the bundle descends to the rack, the ropes are unhooked and the grass can be spread on poles where it will dry in about a week, rain or shine!

We use the same rope set-up but without the landing rack, when putting dry hay in the lower portion of the barn. The team can lift almost a third of a ton to a sling. When it is high enough to swing across the barn, I start to back the horses. The hay swings right to the back wall if everything works right and that saves a great deal of time and toil. The team can unload a wagon load of hay in 10 minutes, including time for taking the ropes off each of the three sling loads. The horses are then hitched back on the wagon and are ready to go out into the field for another load.

When we first started here we cut grass with a scythe, raking it up with hand rakes, then hauling it on a stoneboat with a hay rack on it. We soon came to the conclusion a wagon was essential. The one we acquired is an ancient affair with wooden wheels and steel tires which get loose every time the wood shrinks. New shims must be driven in between the sections of wood to tighten them or the tires will fall off.

Our next acquisition was a five-foot mower and finally we obtained a ten-foot rake. One implement a year was all we could afford. All this equipment was taken apart and loaded on pack horses. The main frame of the mower couldn't be reduced to a lighter piece than 160 pounds so we had to put it up on the horse in such a way that part of it was on the center of the saddle and 100 pounds was over the side, balancing it. Thuja, the ever-patient, long-suffering black mare took this load as she had endured so many other miserable ones.

A gas washing machine was one of our later purchases. Jack carried it on his own back. We removed everything we could, wringer and motor, but could not get the heavy gears off the bottom, so it still weighed about 90 pounds. Jack had to walk bent over almost horizontal from his hips in order not to be pulled over backwards with the wide pack. Susan led Rommy on the days Jack carried the washer and I had the other three horses. He did not try to pack it all the way from Atnarko to Stillwater in one day, but took it in four stages.

As we live 20 miles from the end of even the semblance of a road and 25 miles from the part of it fit for trucks and cars, we must horse pack and raft in almost everything we buy. We try to get all the heavy supplies in at one time because it is not easy to take horses down except when the rafts are assembled for the fall packing. It is much faster and easier to move freight and horses across the lake on rafts than to make them pack all those tons of supplies around, especaiily as neither the trail around Lonesome nor Stillwater is very good.

The new raft gave us 6,500 pounds freight capacity, together with a load of four horses. With the 10 h.p. motor churning at full throttle, the run from the foot of the lake to the head where the mud flats begin, requires only about 90 minutes.

Some years the water was high enough for us to run the raft up the 400 or 500 feet of shallow river channel right to the grain shed but in the fall of 1969 the water was so low we had to transfer the entire 160 sacks, weighing 100 pounds each, into the boat, then tow the heavily laden craft up the channel to the shed. Each load required about five boat trips between raft and shed to get it unloaded.

In 1961 we built a raft of cedar and spruce logs especially for Stillwater, using spruce under the impression it wouldn't waterlog as quickly as cedar. In a very few years, despite the fact all the logs were hauled out and left on skids as soon as the packing job was completed, the spruce logs rotted. That raft was replaced in 1966 with TX Mary P., built to carry 6,500 pounds of freight.

The lake this raft works on is known as Snag Lake to us. After rushing out of Lonesome Lake the Atnarko River is boiling with rapids for a couple of miles, then slows for another mile before creating what used to be an area of almost still water meandering through grass swamps and meadows to a shallow lake about two-and-a-half miles long. This was once a beautiful area of green meadows, dark green pine-clad hillsides and clean water. It formed an important feeding area for trumpeter swans as well as many ducks and geese in spring and fall. Otter, beaver and mink also live there. Grizzly bear and timber wolves gorge themselves along the muddy banks after the sockeye and spring salmon spawn in the fall. In the course of land clearing by the old method of setting fires and allowing them to burn over large areas, the place became a scene of barren desolation, black stubs of trees and bare rocks. In November, 1936, a flood caused the Stillwater to rise eight feet, creating a body of water filled with stumps and snags, dangerous to navigation. The level of water is now shallow enough again to provide a good feeding area for the swans. Sedimentation and the washing out of the dam has pretty well restored the area for this purpose.

In the fall of 1961, Jack packed in on his back enough marine grade fir plywood to build our very own boat for Lonesome Lake. We didn't like borrowing boats all the time. The new boat is large and stable enough to haul a ton of freight if the water is calm and deep enough to float it. Phalarope has a planing hull so with one person and the 10 h.p. Mercury, she skims along at 30 m.p.h., just riding on the last third of the keel.

The following year we built a smaller boat, Tern, which can be easily rowed, although we generally use a 2½ h.p. Johnson Seahorse I bought in 1947.

We also constructed a small cabin on a flat along the river for temporary storage of freight. My brother Stanley owns the land which he allows us to use for the purpose.

A year after we were married, we installed a telephone system between Fogswamp and The Birches. My parents purchased the phones and we provided the mile-and-a-half of wire and strung it. We used it a lot in the days when we were helping them with all work requiring horses. At that time, as now, we had the only ones in the valley. Now there is a tractor at The Birches and we do none of their horse work. Susan uses the phone a fair amount to talk to her grandmother.

In 1970, the old Venturi Bridge was hauled down and the Highbank, a sturdier and higher bridge on which to cross the Atnarko, was built on our own land.

7

Trails and Roads

By now it will be obvious that the use of trails to get from one place to another is central to the lives of all of us who live at Fogswamp Farm and The Birches.

Even with the development of local airlines, the situation has not altered all that much. For one thing, the radio phone at the Edwards'place is in a location of fringe reception and that very often means no messages go either way. There are other times when only one of the persons on the line can hear the conversation and there is no way to ask questions or clarify messages. This leads to confusion and the eventual outcome becomes uncertain, to put it mildly! Additionally, of course, the use of commercial planes is expensive.

A description of our main trails and roads, their history and development, is therefore important.

Alexander Mackenzie crossed the North American continent, started down the Fraser River, then travelled overland to the Bella Coola valley. Here he borrowed Indian dugout canoes and floated down the Bella Coola River to the head of North Bentinck Arm in 1793, becoming the first white man to reach there. In 1864 the first settlers, Norwegians, founded the village of Bella Coola at the mouth of the river. These people built their own roads from farm to farm and from the inlet. Indians used the river for a road as far as Stuie and had pack trails leading out of the valley to the Chilcotin Plateau. They caught and smoked the sockeye and other salmon for food and probably horse packed some fish back to the Chilcotin.

In about 1914 the first automobile came to the valley. It was a great day and everyone talked about it. A lot of horses doubtless had their wits scared out of them in those early days.

The end of the original road remained one mile east of Stuie at Belarco for several years after it reached there in 1929. Apparently the people working on it lacked the requisite ambition so far from "town" and it took them four years to produce a single mile of road across an almost dead level stretch of sand, covered with small lodgepole pine. Although they had a bulldozer to smash out the next few miles, roadbuilding stalled again until around 1943 when more advances were made in an easterly direction adding a few more miles of rough, narrow road. It wasn't much better than the horse trail it followed, but at least a truck could run over it.

The Post Office Department brought mail to Atnarko twice a month in those days, either on horseback or snowshoes. There was a Post Office in Atnarko for a number of years. In the early '50s they "improved" the service by terminating deliveries at a place known as Firvale, 26 miles farther from us. At the time it didn't matter too much to the residents of Lonesome Lake as we brought the mail in by Taylorcraft but when my father moved away with the plane, we were obliged to bring our mail in over the trail.

A kind family, Mr. and Mrs. Gordon Corbould, bring it to Tweedsmuir Lodge at Stuie, 36 miles away. That walk is sometimes made partly by snowshoes in winter but in summer it is cut to 26 miles by the use of boats. About ten miles of that is pretty strenuous walking, the trail leading over talus slopes and through heavily wooded areas where there are frequently windfalls to climb over and under. There are also a number of boulder-filled, fast-running creeks to be crossed. The travelling becomes somewhat easier once we get to the old road at Hotnarko although by the time we reach the often deserted highway we are always willing to accept a ride, should one come along. Jack alone tends to get more offers of rides than the whole family does. Three people with bulging packs makes an imposing load for anything but an empty pickup!

In the fall of 1972 we acquired bicycles for use on the road between Stuie and Young Creek, a gravel stretch not really very suitable for bikes. It does save several hours walking on each trip however, and the backpacks can be attached to the carriers and baskets.

Each year as the road edged closer to Lonesome Lake our hopes rose that it would go through the Hotnarko valley and connect to a road from Anahim Lake in the Chilcotin country. However, in 1953 they sent the cat up Tsedakuko River, killing our hopes for a road up Hotnarko, which would have been about eight miles closer to us. There wasn't enough money to construct the shorter but costlier route since there is a three- or four-mile stretch in Hotnarko River which is a real box canyon and would have required extensive blasting.

In the early years people managed to make a horse trail over all the miles of talus and bypassed the cliffs by putting in switchbacks up out of the Hotnarko Canyon. A lot of the trail was built up by the simple process of rolling and heaving large broken rocks over the edge of the trail then filling the holes between with smaller stuff until a level trail two or three feet wide resulted. Horses must wear shoes, of course, but at least there is never trouble with mud on this kind of trail.

People who took up pre-emptions at Stillwater worked on the trail from Hotnarko River to Stillwater some time before World War I. As there is a granite cliff rising steeply right from Atnarko's rocky bed to several hundred feet, these people elected to throw a big bridge across the river just at the start of the bluff. Since the river was in a number of channels further upstream, more bridges were needed to return the trail to the east side of the valley. These smaller ones did not last long but the big one stood until an extra high water in June of 1948 shifted the stringers off the piers and carried them away on roily waves.

With the bridges gone, the settlers decided to put a trail over the bluff and by doing a small amount of blasting were able to get a "passable trail" over the cliff about 150 feet above the river. If the foreman on that job hadn't been so cocksure he could blast solid granite without drilling, the trail might have gone around the face of the bluff on a level. There would have been a rock cut about 100 feet or so long, but it would have meant a far better trail. There are some compensations to the existing one, though, as long as you aren't carrying a heavy pack. When you get to the top of the climb the view is almost worth the effort.

Mt. Ada, to the south, rears its head up in the middle of the valley while to the north and west one can see a long way down the spectacular valley. In the fall the colors are magnificent as there are a lot of cottonwood trees in the valley along the river, creating a brilliant yellow splash in that season. Further along the bluff they had to cross another section of smooth granite, about 20 feet wide. Instead of putting in a rock cut, they built a small bridge across the 45 degree sloping face of the cliff. This bridge served for about 16 years until a rock fall carried it to the roaring river below. Luckily there was a narrow ledge left a few feet up the bluff where a person could walk around. I aswas able, in 1948, to lead a seven-month-old Ayrshire bull calf around on this ledge although he had to kind of lean against the cliff face at one point where a chunk of rock jutted out and left little room for sure footing.

In the fall of that year a two-foot-wide rock cut was put in— and this should continue to serve unless there is some tremendous cataclysm and the entire mountain tumbles into the river.

To the casual reader, a two-foot-wide trail across a cliff-face may seem inadequate for packed horses, but the cliff slopes away at a 45 degree angle, leaving ample room for a pack or a ten-gallon drum of gas on each side of a horse. It would be too bad if the horse hit a drum on the rocks as the sudden deceleration might cause its back legs to swing around off the edge of the trail and send the horse sliding down to the river. It would be difficult indeed to get the animal back onto the trail. For that reason we use our most careful horse for drums or boxes.

Many sections of the trail along the river are lavishly decorated with large dead spring salmon in the fall when we are packing. Some of the bodies are so delicate and fragrant our horses are very careful to step around them, not wanting to have the mass of stinking liquid squirt up their legs.

As the trappers travelled up the valley south of Stillwater to trap, they had some sort of trail along the river for about two miles but as the river is unsuitable for mink, they left it and followed the path of least resistance across the rocky Douglas fir timbered delta of Lake Creek, across the open boulder bars and so to the foot of Lonesome Lake. We follow that route to this day except for minor alterations due to the propensities of the creek for changing its channels from year to year. The three-mile section of trail between Stillwater and Lonesome Lake runs on the west side of the valley and is on river level most of the way except for two short climbs of about 15 feet. The trail winds through some of the highest and darkest forest where Douglas firs tower as high as 130 feet with almost half the trunk clear to the first branches. They are only about two feet in diameter but stand close to one another, creating some beautiful stands. Tall, straight cedars and cottonwoods are interspersed with the firs. Little direct sunlight ever penetrates to the forest floor so there is not much undergrowth except a few anaemic cedars and in the fall, various species of fungi.

I believe my father expanded the old trap trail to make it fit for horses sometime in the '20s. In 1926 he cut a horse trail around the west side of Lonesome Lake for five miles, then swam his horses across a narrow place in the lake. The trail continued on the east side to his farm. Due to an early freeze-up in the fall of 1941, the Edwards' horses could not be swum at the narrows as usual so a rough trail was scratched out of the rocky hillside the rest of the way to the south end of Lonesome Lake on the west side. This is a poor piece of trail with rough footing and many short, steep pitches to get over or under small outcrops and cliffs.

There has been a trail along the west side of Big Lagoon for years and also one leading to Elbow Lake where the Edwards' stock was put to range and my father did some trapping. This passes by our place and marks the end of the job if we are on a supply-packing expedition.

For a number of years while we were transporting grain, it took as much as three truckloads to bring it and our supplies to the junction of the Tsedakuk and Atnarko Rivers where the reasonably good road ends. It was left piled there, covered with plastic and gradually hauled by wagon and packhorse three miles to Atnarko, where it was stored in a cabin. The job of getting the load as far as that generally took around a week and if all went according to plan, anywhere between two and three weeks to move grain and supplies to the north end of Stillwater, where it was again temporarily stored. It still had to be moved another three miles to the north end of Lonesome Lake, a project involving a number of horse-packing trips. At the end of all this, it was "merely" a matter of two or three trips across the six miles of Lonesome Lake at which point the grain was finally stored in the grain boxes leaving us only the job of packing a ton or so of our supplies to the south end of Big Lagoon where it was packed or wagoned to the house!

Sometimes the horses were brought up the lake before the last trips of freight were rafted up. At other times the horses were left at the foot of the lake and the freight took priority. If the lake froze, the horses could manage to walk around the shore a lot easier than 18,000 pounds of supplies could!

The last major job of the year consists of dismantling the TX Mary P. on Stillwater and hauling it out one log at a time just prior to the final pack to Lonesome Lake, then dismantling the TX Balsa in the same manner and hauling it out at the conclusion of the packing job.

When we began the trip in September of 1969 we weren't quite sure if there'd be a trail at all in one section. A D7 cat was smashing out a road up the valley somewhere between the Hotnarko River and the Atnarko. It was never intended as a permanent road, just as a route for surveyors to use while laying out a super highway somewhere in someone's distant dream.

When we got about a mile downstream of Hotnarko River, we heard the cat working along the base of a rockslide and blocking the trail with a huge ridge of rock and dirt. Susan and I held the five horses and one steer while Jack went ahead to let the cat skinner know we were there. Meantime, hordes of blackflies did their best to devour all of us.

The cat skinner very kindly bulldozed down the barrier enough for us to get over it. Some of the horses had seen a cat only very briefly the year before yet none of them was upset by the huge clanking yellow monster. Later on we took the horses past the cat as it was in motion, pushing a great blade full of dirt towards the piece of road we were walking on. Each horse gave the monster a suspicious glare as it passed.

One day we were returning to Atnarko from Stillwater and had stopped all the horses except Thuja, who always went loose on the trail. We were waiting for the cat skinner to finish a piece of work he was doing. Thuja seemed to want a closer look at it and wandered ahead until she got so near the machine we became concerned about the rockslide coming down on her and Jack strode up to drag her back to safety.

For 10 days we passed that cat twice a day as we made our round trip packing goods. In the afternoon we would pass the cat skinner's truck, two or three surveyors' trucks and a line truck. Half-an-hour later all this traffic overtook and had to pass us! This generally occurred on a rockslide area where the road was narrow and not one of our nags appeared to realize a truck couldn't get round them. What was worse, each seemed to think if his or her front feet were off the road, that would suffice. As the side of the road was rough, none of them wanted to get out of the smooth part so we ended up having to turn them all around and lead them past the truck, then continue on down the road after the truck had started on!

As the road advanced up the valley, garbage followed. A liquor bottle propped in soft sand had been shot several times. The resulting mess of broken glass so enraged me it was a good thing the person who had done it wasn't still around. Later the same day, as we climbed to where the road crosses Sugar Camp Creek, we saw a camper parked in the middle of the road. A young man lounged on the tailgate, gun in hand. In the creek was a can full of what appeared to be bullet holes. On the side of the road was another bottle, shattered into sharp spears.

From the evidence, he must have been shooting lengthwise along the road and into the water on the other side of a rise. A person approaching wouldn't be seen until his head appeared in the line of fire. With difficulty I managed to contain my anger.

The possibility of a road coming closer can obviously be considered a mixed blessing.

* * * * *

87

8

Lonesome Lake, February 15, 1976

Today I learned something of the physical cost of living in the wilderness. Having experienced just a little of the hardship of having to walk everywhere over fairly rough trails, I've been trying to stretch my imagination to envision bringing home enough groceries (and everything else) for a period of *four years*. My mind reels at the idea of bringing it all in over that distance—without wheels.

Shopping and back-packing goods in used to be a yearly job for the family but after they stopped packing grain in for the swans, they had only their own needs to consider so they tried extending the period to every other year. Finding that feasible, the Turners decided to lengthen the times between supply purchasing even further. They are currently more than half-way through the first four year period and are feeling optimistic that at least everything crucial will last out.

The idea of being so well organized that one could shop so infrequently simply boggles the mind. Particularly when one bears in mind that one cannot just run down to the cornerstore to pick up any little item that may have been forgotten. Not when the nearest corner store is an exhausting 56 miles distant.

For the benefit of anyone with a yen to get away from it all and who would like some idea of what it takes to disappear for four years, the Turner shopping list follows.

Just a warning, however. This list is only valid if the refugee is prepared to provide quite a long list of items through the hard work of home production. These include the wide range of fruit and vegetables mentioned in Trudy's account of their garden, together with nearly all their fish, meat and dairy products. Trudy puts up a total of 300-350 quarts of produce annually.

Now for the "grocery list"—supplies for three people (plus stock and pets) for four years.

1200 lbs. flour
1000 lbs. sugar (includes canning needs)
25 lbs. macaroni
20 lbs. dried beans
20 lbs. dried peas
40 lbs. rolled oats
30 lbs. Red River cereal
40 lbs. rice
30 lbs. baking powder
50 lbs. brown sugar
30 lbs. icing sugar
40 lbs. powdered laundry soap
80 bars face soap
10 - 8 oz. tins. yeast
16 lbs. honey
64 oz. vanilla
30 lbs. corn meal
20 lbs. raisins
1 gallon vinegar
12 lbs. corn starch
8 lbs. cocoa
120 lbs. table salt (also used in canning meat and produce)
40 lbs. dairy salt (for butter)
40 oz. table molasses
20 tins concentrated lemon juice
20 lbs. dried prunes and figs
10 lbs. barley
6 lbs. tapioca
30 bottles Certo
Spices and herbs: 4 tins each of pepper, sage, savory, thyme, hamburger seasoning, bay leaves, cinnamon, mace, cloves,

nutmeg, paprika, allspice and ginger.
4 bottles each of almond and maple extract
4 cartons match packets
1 dozen pot cleaners
2 tins Bon Ami
24 rolls toilet paper (mostly in lieu of facial tissues... the classic Eaton's catalogue was what I found in "The White House," at least until I reminded them of what a collector's item they were using so frivolously!)
300 lbs. block salt for cattle
100 lbs. grain salt for cattle
200 lbs. dry meal dog food
300 lbs. garden fertilizer
100 lbs. grass fertilizer

Depending on the financial situation at the time the shopping expedition takes place, the following items may or may not be purchased:

Cherry jam, tinned pineapple, apricots, mushroom soup, pears, peaches, tinned clams, dates, walnuts, corn syrup, dry fruit for cakes, glazed cherries, granola, selection of prepared cereals, dry cheese, peanut butter, marmalade, malted milk powder, dehydrated soups, custard powders, drink powders and meat pastes.

If that isn't enough to check over carefully before setting off, there's another list which they go over to discover what residual supplies are currently on hand and what jobs are contemplated before adding them to the shopping list.
This consists of the following:

horseshoes and nails
lumber
gas and kerosene
outboard and 10 and 30 weight chainsaw oil
building nails
pine tar
animal medications
human medications
stove and lamp parts
ammunition
clothes and boots

radio and flashlight batteries
sewing machine oil, thread and needles
sheets, pillow cases and linens
garden chemicals
rope
paint and creosote
preserving jars, lids and rings
writing paper and envelopes
pen refills
photographic supplies
axe handles
files
grass and garden seeds
insect repellent
tooth paste and tooth brushes
sanitary pads
machine grease
mop sponges
broom
horse oats
powdered eggs
chicken feed
Prague powder for meat preserving
baking soda.

Most Christmas gifts are made at the house from natural or available materials but any store-bought purchases must be ordered in August so they can be brought in at the end-of-October mail trip.

The British Columbia library has given the Turners the special privileges accorded isolated users. A total of eight books, four for Susan and four for her parents, can be kept for twelve weeks instead of the usual six. A catalogue was sent to them from which they selected categories in which they were most interested. Regularly, a list of available books in these categories is sent to them so they can make their choices. The books are sent from Victoria, postage paid.

Although the building and extension of new roads has now cut the pack trail length by eight miles, a weak bridge and a possible washout threatens to make the entire trip necessary once more. In any event, the project is an awe-inspiring one, particularly to city-dwellers.

It must be understood that the Turner diet tends to vary over the seasons, with a concentration on high protein during the winter before the meat can spoil with the advent of warmer spring weather and a preponderance of fresh fruit and vegetables during summer and fall. The full range of food is available over the course of the entire year, but fresh fruit, meat and vegetables are all more flavorful and enjoyable than canned ones. At any rate, the diet must balance itself out as the Turners have an enviable health record.

Taking into consideration the immense difficulty of getting out of the valley, I queried them about health and dental records.

Trudy herself has been to the doctor only for Susan's birth and to the dentist to have some teeth pulled. Jack's only medical problem has been wood slivers, "And I cut them out," said Trudy. He has had a couple of cracked bones over the years but they have healed themselves. Susan—"She doesn't even get slivers," laughed her mother. She has paid two visits to the dentist but no work was required.

The Turners admit it isn't all a case of good luck. Fully aware of the hazards of living in their circumstances, plus the problems of getting out, every member of the family tends to be very careful and prudent and no one takes unnecessary risks.

Although the airline will come in to pick up a passenger any time weather permits, communications can and do break down.

The Turners have become pretty skilful veterinarians over the years, through sheer necessity. The animals have suffered many more minor and serious injuries than the humans on the place. Four horses have had wounds requiring surgery, a cow occasionally retains her afterbirth and chickens get attacked by predators every so often.

The Turners repeatedly aver there is nothing heroic in what they are doing and since they are there strictly by their own choice and preference, one would have to agree. At the same time, there is room for a great deal of admiration for their ability to organize their lives and for the high degree of self-reliance the family has achieved.

9

Weather and Watermelons

Fogswamp Farm has a mixture of Interior and Coast weather. Sometimes during the winter we have temperatures as high as 60°F above with 50 m.p.h. winds right off the coast. On the other extreme we can get a mass of Arctic air funnelling down the valley from the Interior, either from Charlotte Lake or down the Hotnarko Valley. Then the mercury plummets to 20° or 30°F. The coldest temperature recorded at Fogswamp during the past twenty years was -34°F but during the winter of 1949-50 it dropped to -46°F in the Atnarko valley.

Even when a cold spell prevails, the coast influence modifies the deep cold which is being experienced just 25 to 30 miles to the east. In that area they frequently get lows of -50° to -60°F. These cold spells do not normally occur more than three or four times during a winter. Each one lasts a week or so, the extreme being a period of low temperatures persisting for a month without letup. Even in 1968-69, when there was a six-week period of cold weather, it was broken by a week of warm weather when rain fell for three days and the temperature climbed to the 30s. By using all the morning temperatures for the entire six-week period, an average of -7°F was reached.

A cold spell almost always ends with a warm storm out of the Gulf of Alaska. When the warm air gets to this area it comes howling up Knight Inlet and sometimes within 24

95

hours, will drive the temperature up from about -20°F to 48°F and the pouring rain will melt the snow.

Snow usually comes around the end of November but might not stay on the ground until Christmas. Warm rain and wind often removes much of the snow as soon as it falls. After Christmas the most severe cold spell of the winter is likely to occur and the snow builds up. The most snow we have had here was five feet in 1974. Most winters the maximum is about a foot. Although more in inches may actually fall, a lot of it gets rained off or compacted. Sometimes the snow stays until mid-April but more often starts to melt off by mid-February and is gone by the first of April. One year the ground went bare in January and only an inch or so of snow fell for the remainder of the season. If the snow is still on the ground in February, a hard crust forms on top, frequently strong enough to support the weight of a full-grown Hereford bull.

As spring advances and more snow melts, the creeks and rivers start to rise. Full high water is not reached until sometime in June as a rule. The delayed melt from the six to eight thousand foot peaks which rise from the timbered 3,500 foot plateau, causes the late high water.

The first real signs of spring are the simultaneous arrival of the Rocky Mountain bluebird and great clouds of yellow alder pollen blowing across the fields. On the south coast, buds begin to swell in March but don't actually open for a month. Here, beginning to swell in late April, they spend only a week or so opening.

In early May yellow drifts of pine pollen are seen along the hillsides on windy days while the water willows bloom with inch-long yellow amments sweet with nectar, attracting swarms of bees. Gooseberries bloom with shooting-star-shaped purple flowers and the Rufous hummingbirds arrive and begin working the nectar-laden blossoms. Quaking aspens grow up most talus slopes along the lake shores and are the first to start to leaf out in spring as well as the last to go bare each fall. In early May the aspens turn a light silvery green as their buds begin to burst in the steadily increasing warmth from the sun as it strikes the rocks at a steep angle, warming them so that they emanate heat throughout the night as well.

The first boat trip down Lonesome Lake each spring is an experience comparable with that of entering a new and

96

unexplored country, although actually I know it as well as my own kitchen. There is the new-alive, sweet smell of cottonwoods and the odor of damp earth after the winter's snow has gone.

By the end of July most of the mountainsides above timberline are bare and wild flowers are profuse in the short, hot growing season. Summers are usually moderate with the high being about 85°F in the shade. Nights are cool, morning temperatures ranging between 45° to 50°F through the summer months. There is frost during May and part of June but rarely more until late August and sometimes September. Some summers are dry with very little rain while others will be so wet that weeds prosper.

Early fall is usually a pleasant time of year. I recall boating across Lonesome Lake one memorable October when it was beautiful beyond words. There was not a breath of wind to mar the mirror surface of the lake. A few cumulus clouds, resembling little gobs of white wool, drifted slowly across a delicate blue sky. It was afternoon and as the boat sped across the surface, fragmenting the reflections in the water, it threw up a sheet of fine spray, creating a double rainbow on each side of the boat. For five miles the rainbows followed us, until we changed direction at the north end of Big Lagoon. Jack cut the motor and let the boat drift until the water smoothed. He then took pictures of the perfect autumn colors. As the nights had been warm until just a few days previously, the birches and cottonwoods had remained green unusually late. It took just a couple of frosty nights to turn every leaf a vivid yellow. This glowing hue along the lake and up the mountains was faithfully mirrored in the water. Just as Jack finished photographing natural beauty, a Cessna 180, also wearing fall colors, glided gracefully onto the glassy surface of the lagoon, amidst a great shower of spray.

After a pleasant early autumn, the dull and rainy days which follow are brightened only by the golden foliage which turns the mountain waterways into vivid streaks of color. A little later the leaves are gone, snow has already moved to below timberline and the trumpeter swans start to arrive at their winter home. Soon after this the lakes begin to freeze over, heralding the start of another winter.

This is not a bad season here either. It is time for rest for many living things, a time to restore moisture to the parched earth, a time of hearing timber wolves and trumpeter swans. It is only in winter I can afford to sit and relax enough to paint a picture or write a story, or to read books there was no opportunity to dip into during the busy summer months. It is a time of roast beef and grilled steak, of mellow afternoons and soft, snowy moonlit nights.

Winter is also when many incredible ice sculptures appear in small creeks. When a branch dangles down close to the water, small drops of spray freeze to it and create a huge bell-like ball which floats on the surface and swings to and fro in the current. The accretion of ice, built up drop by drop, may be a foot or more across and climb up the branch an equal distance. These ice formations can weigh 50 pounds, yet be attached to a branch only three-quarters of an inch through. They usually become frozen fast to the ever-widening shore ice at this point.

A positively spectacular display was found hanging from a log lying over a small stream. The log was about three feet above the water but spray jumping up had formed icicles about a foot long and four inches apart along the length of it. Three or four cross bars connected these and supported several tiny icicles. The resultant filigree was so delicate it looked as though someone had painstakingly cut it out with a coping saw.

There is a surprising amount of color to be seen during the cold season. When alder and birch trees are wet after a frosty night and the sun shines brightly, melting the frost, all the small twigs and dormant buds and amments appear brownish-purple. Red osier dogwood becomes a more vivid dark red and the marginal willows by the river a particularly intense reddish yellow when they are wet. When the weather turns really cold, cedar leaves become blackish and shrink within themselves. The two junipers we transplanted into our yard turn a dark, purplish-green and the balsam fir provides a contrast by remaining the same bluish-green regardless of temperature.

The valley floor is covered with fair-sized Douglas fir, cedar, lodgepole pine, birth, spruce, cottonwoods, willow and quaking aspen together with a small amount of maple. These trees all contribute to the attractiveness of our surroundings and serve in the development of the farm as well. There are good cedars for shakes and boards, young cedar and fir for fence rails and construction, plus maple for anything requiring strength.

There are wild flowers, wild raspberries and devil's club, that thorny monster plant of rich, moist areas, as well as green ground cover of a variety of types too numerous to list.

Local animal life includes deer, grizzly and black bear, moose, otter, foxes, coyotes, mink, marten, weasels, lynx, cougar, wolves, beaver and most of the small rodents that make a nuisance around a farm. The bears are there mostly during the fall months when the sockeye salmon are spawning and dying and the bears are building fat for their winter sleep. The results of their feasts on rotten salmon are large, odorferous, gray, slimy "pies" strewn along the trails at frequent intervals!

Only the odd doe spends summers in the valley. Most deer retire to higher levels in late spring and do not return until feed becomes covered with deep snow, usually in November. They tend to come where people are clearing land and knocking down Douglas fir, birch and cedar trees in the process. They eat the greenery from these and the twigs of birch trees. Cedar is their favorite tree and they survive most of the winter on this, together with fir needles and black moss. This moss grows on dead trees and branches to a length of nearly a foot. Snow and wind bring down dead trees and branches with this edible stuff on them. Deer will willingly eat hay if given a chance, which we don't provide as we need all the hay we grow for our stock.

Most of our hay crop is comprised of tame grasses and several kinds of clover. Timothy does well here. All crops need fertilizer to make good growth. All the manure from the stock, as well as several hundred pounds of commercial fertilizer, is used to produce the 20 tons of hay we harvest annually.

Having a relatively mild climate, we are able to grow most of the ordinary vegetables and fruits. Some of the more tender plants must have special treatment. We always start tomatoes, squash and cabbage during March and April in boxes in the house. When the weather warmed up, we used to set them out in the garden. This gave them a better start, but we still found our tomatoes didn't ripen before frosts came along. In the spring of 1966 we tried a new wrinkle.

We constructed a 22x5-foot cold frame using cedar logs with a top made of four frames covered with clear plastic, hinged at the bottoms so they can be raised or lowered. If the sun is shining the roof is opened to allow heat to escape but on dull or rainy days the roof allows the temperature to rise at least 15 degrees above the outside. The lengthened growing season allowed us to get ripe tomatoes off the vine that year, a real luxury. The following year we transplanted the young tomatoes into the frame May 15 and they did very well. We enjoyed ripe fruit in early August that year and have continued to do so each year since.

All tender plants must be protected from frosts both in spring and fall. We do this by placing gunny sacks over the plants any night frost threatens. This is a time-consuming job and one we are reluctant to do after the plants are big enough to bloom as the coverings appear to harm the flowers, especially those of tomatoes. Corn gets nipped with frost at times but can regrow from the roots, as can potatoes if their first leaves are frost-killed.

With the tomatoes doing so well in the cold frame we decided to try peppers, cantaloupes and watermelons in one as well. In a slightly smaller edition of the tomato house, we were successful.

We sow hardy seedlings like celery and onions the first of May. We tried planting greens that early but the white-crowned and yellow-crowned sparrows come through about that time and consumed every radish, beet or sprig of chard that had put in an appearance. We used to wait until they left, a week or so later, but got impatient to taste a new vegetable so decided to foil them by placing pieces of chicken wire over the seedlings until the birds departed.

Potatoes, some carrots, onions, corn fodder, peavine, beans and turnips are harvested by mid-September. Beets, mangles and parsnips and some cabbage may be left in the garden until November or even later for savoy cabbage. The squash and pumpkins are put in the house in early September to finish ripening. Tomatoes are brought in and put on wire racks hung from the kitchen ceiling if they are still green when we have to leave on a packing trip. They ripen in about a month, depending on how near to ripe they are when put up.

Our garden covers one fifth of an acre. We have a large raspberry patch and 12 rhubarb plants which produce far too much for just the three of us. Some of our rhubarb stalks are two inches wide and twenty inches long. Two leaves laid head to tail cover a square yard! We also have a fair-sized strawberry bed, a few blackberries which produce a magnificent crop of thorns, and a good number of asparagus plants.

We enjoy flowers so there is always some ground given to this "useless" crop. Gladiolus is the most conspicuous flower we raise. My mother gave me a couple of bulbs several years ago and now I have enough to plant half the garden.

Most flowers are, of course, produced during warm weather but in the winter of 1968 I collected one of the most gorgeous specimens imaginable, and of a most unique variety—an ice flower. Its six-inch base was attached to the surface of a frozen-over pool in the creek where it tumbled down the hill. From here the flower rose 16 inches into the air. A delicate shell of ice tapered to a rounded top, its entire surface clad in cream-colored frost crystals. It weighed only about two pounds. I gently broke the flower loose from the ice, carried it home and carefully placed it over one of the pickets in front of the house where it remained for about ten days before the sun dissolved its fragile beauty.

We grow enough peas and beans, both green and shell as well as corn, to put up about 120 quarts annually. We try to raise sweet corn each year but even using the fastest and earliest varieties on the market, we find many summers are just too cool for it to ripen enough to can before frost. To overcome the shortage we raise an early nonsweet corn and although the flavor is not comparable and it is tougher, it is not too bad when canned. We use the sweet corn fresh later in the fall after it has ripened sufficiently on drying racks in the barn. It's not as good as fresh corn from the garden but still better than some we've purchased in stores. Energy in the stems goes to ripen the corn kernels once they are set. If left on the stalks long enough the ears will become fully ripe.

We also preserve a supply of meat. This is mostly our own home-raised beef, but occasionally there will be some venison as well. We put some meat into a salt solution and this gives us fresh meat for a longer period. We have no means of refrigeration here except in winter and that is so undependable no food can be counted on to remain frozen once the weather begins to warm up. We make some of our fat beef into bacon—not as good as pork, but decidedly cheaper!

We even can milk in jars. Since there was no information on this in our canning books, we wrote to the Department of Agriculture, but to no avail. We set about to experiment until we found a method which made milk safe to drink and didn't completely ruin the flavor. We pour fresh milk into jars, put on the rubber rings, glass lids and screw bands. We then place them in a pressure cooker with a couple of quarts of water in it. With the lid on, it is allowed to heat and blow off steam for seven minutes for the 7-quart or nine minutes for the 14-quart cooker. The steam valve is then closed, pressure brought up to five pounds and the cooker removed from the heat immediately to allow pressure to return to zero. We then take out the jars and screw down the bands. This provides us with preserved milk which tastes much like canned Pacific milk. We have used it with no ill effects for as long as a year-and-a-half after canning. It must be kept out of the light as much as possible, as direct sunlight will ruin the flavor of any milk in about five minutes. We use this product when the cow must dry off for her rest period.

A word of warning, however. People canning milk by this method do so at their own risk! I accept no responsibility for any trouble they may have.

We make our own butter whenever the cow is giving a sufficient quantity of milk. It requires around 80 pounds of milk, or four milkings, to produce four pounds of sweet butter. If I have lots of milk and am trying to make a quantity of butter for the packing job, I separate the milk with the Swedish separator. With just a relatively small amount, I hand-skim it and churn smaller batches of thinner cream. The churn is also of Swedish manufacture and is extremely efficient, churning even very thin cream, if it is 62°F and in only a very few minutes.

When I was a young lass at home my mother used to fill a quart jar half-full of cream and tell me to churn it. I would take it, sit on a chair and patiently bang the jar on my knee for half-an-hour or so before the sloshy contents turned to butter. Half-an-hour, that is, if I was lucky. More often than not the cream would be just as thin at the end of that time as when I started. Sometimes I'd pound the thing on my battered knee for an hour or two before it would reluctantly coagulate. Then I think it "came" only because all the time the jar was wearing out my knee, the cream was also getting warmer until finally the fat globules had no choice but to stick together in a soft unctuous mass. When churning by this method, butter was scarcely worth the effort. My people got hold of a Swedish churn just before I got married and since theirs was clearly more efficient than a jar, we also purchased one. Our model is the smallest one made and will churn up to three quarts of cream. It had to be purchased directly from Sweden as there was no company handling them in Canada at that time.

In the fall of 1959 we brought in half-a-dozen New Hampshire pullets. They didn't lay until they were eight months old. When we were packing during autumn of the following year, they were all eaten up by something. As the red hens were such poor layers, and my mother was raising leghorns, we got some pullets from her. These are completely white birds with large, floppy red combs. They begin laying when four or five months old and go on throughout the year unless sub-zero weather freezes their big crimson combs. If this happens they stop laying until recovered.

During the winter of 1968-69 we had a severe cold spell. Two of the hens selected that time to change feathers and suddenly appeared naked as pan-ready fryers! The house they live in is unheated and has very little ability to hold even the limited warmth provided by four hens. Being afraid they would freeze, I built a cage for them in the house.

As the cold spell went on, another one decided to moult. That meant three hens in the house and since we could hardly leave one alone, we ended up with all four sharing our quarters. They ate off and on through the night. Even in total darkness we would hear the slow tap-tap of their beaks picking up feed from the cage floor. They were given names and became quite friendly during their visit. One of them, Brenda, would start talking to me as soon as I returned from the swan-feeding trip each morning. As they did not smell very good, we hustled them back to their own house as soon as it warmed up sufficiently. Living in the house and eating well gave them such a boost they put their new feathers on quickly and were laying about two weeks later.

10

Voices of the Wild

Because we live in the wilderness many people appear to feel we deserve sympathy for the miserable, lonely existence we must lead. At least that's the way it seems from the letters we get.

I'm just continuing to "live in the briar patch" and Jack obviously has no great desire to be "where the action is" or he wouldn't have put forth so much effort to find exactly what he has. I don't miss many of civilization's conveniences. To tell the truth I wouldn't give much of a thanks for store-bought bread, and my family prefers my home-made loaves. About the only thing in the food line we yearn for but cannot provide at Fogswamp is deep-fried prawns!

Our own produce is far more flavorful than anything we've had outside. We even discovered vegetables at the Pacific National Exhibition that weren't as attractive, large or firm as our own.

We don't miss movies either, although we enjoyed such productions as *Mary Poppins* and *Ring of Bright Water* while we were in Vancouver.

Our sympathy goes to the poor harassed city folk who must live in filthy air, walk on concrete and obey the dictates of time and conventions.

Of course, country living has its panics, too, as when Nature runs amuck with an overabundance of rain or snow. But the oft-mentioned "silence of the wilderness" which seems to oppress some people, just does not exist. There are myriad sounds: the call of trumpeter swans overhead, the rush of water, the love-sick wailing of a cat seeking a lover or the loud, insistent bellow of the family cow when her calf is being weaned, not to mention the ever-present undertones of birds. Every season has its distinctive noises.

During winter there is the cheerful and optimistic chitter and "fee-fee" of the black-capped chickadees as they busily tear birch cones apart for the tiny seeds, creating a brown avalanche of discarded scales. They are just as busy when the timber cracks as they are when the cumulus clouds from the southwest sail across the sky and the snow is melting from a 50 degree south wind.

We hear the sometimes musical and sometimes rather harsh notes of the soft-gray whisky jack. These birds will become tame enough, with patience, to come and perch on a hand to eat pieces of fat or meat. They cock their heads on one side, peering intently into your eyes and begin to eat once they decide you aren't going to harm them. They habitually stay all winter and frequently share their food with the larger and more aggressive Clark's nutcracker, mostly because they have no choice. The bossy nutcracker has a beak about three times the length of the jay's and is reluctant to share his food with any other bird.

Depending on the temperature, great horned owls may start hooting in earnest as early as February. The pocket sized pygmy owl starts his effort shortly after. Considering his size, his incessant bell-like call is quite remarkable. I saw one once, sitting on a branch only about 15 feet away, and although I observed him for 10 minutes or more as he turned this way and that, I couldn't for the life of me discern which side of his head was toward me, for he has eye-like markings on the back of his head!

Winter winds create dramatic sounds. One blizzard rattled the frozen branches of the trees along the edge of the field and whistled around the corner of our house, driving fine particles of hard snow onto the window with a gritty sound like sand being thrown against the glass. At the other extreme, strong south winds occasionally howl and roar, warm gusts causing temperatures to shoot up while heat waves dance over the snow and the wind licks it up like a giant starved cat at a saucer of cream. These warm winds seldom produce rain but pick up moisture to such an extent that a six-hour blow of around 30 miles per hour will cause two feet of snow to shrink to a foot without compacting.

After a cold spell all the aspen and birch trees are sheathed in ice, and tinkle in the slightest breeze. The noise made by a tree splitting can be quite loud. Once when the mercury stood at about -20°F, I was hurrying along the trail toward the "swannery" when an eight-inch birch tree nearby split its trunk for a length of eight feet and made a cracking sound that rent the air.

Something is always making some noise, winter or summer, night or day. The trumpeter swans are still here in the late winter when the Canada geese arrive in late February or early March. The last swans don't leave until after the arrival of nearly all the small migratory birds.

In March, when the sun is climbing ever higher each day and the snow is melting into little rivulets, the blue (sooty) grouse begins his hollow hooting. He sits in a tree somewhere up the mountainside and hoots as long as the sun is up. The willow grouse drums on a log day and night starting in late April and carrying on all summer. The varied thrush, a robin-like bird with a prominent black gorget across a bright orange breast and orange bands over his head, is heard on frosty mornings about mid-February. Brewer's blackbirds, shiny black with a white ring around their eyes and a very important pose, "tech-teck" their way from twig to twig along the river. The sombre "tick-tick" of the little junco searching desperately for seeds in the bare ground under the sheds and eaves is soon followed by a hopeful robin yelling "cheer up, cheer up" from the top of a birch or cedar. Then comes the red-winged blackbird, the same color as the brewer's except for a bright red patch on each shoulder. He sits on a branch, hunches his back, opens his beak and contorts his body as though trying to regurgitate a large caterpillar. Ultimately the liquid notes of "o-ka-re-o" emerge, to be repeated frequently throughout the day. Tree swallows swoop across a warm clear sky and dip low over the fields and river, twittering ecstatically. In May, soon after planting time, the yellow-crowned sparrows' solicitous and mocking "oh dear me" can be heard just after they have devoured a row of recently planted seedlings! As the nights get warmer, the hermit thrush rolls his flute-like music across the balmy evenings. A little later he begins his serenade even before daylight brightens the dark alder thicket where he hides. Having got an early start, this elusive ventriloquist often sings all through the day.

On hot afternoons the birds seem to quieten but there are still insects buzzing about, gathering nectar, biting stock or drilling their long slender needles into our flesh! The big, slow snowshoe mosquitoes show up here as early in the year as the middle of February.

To me June is about the nicest month of the year as trees, flowers and grass grow vigorously and a symphony of bird calls fills the air all day and into the late evening.

Robins and varied thrushes linger long after the swans begin to arrive, turning over acres of leaves in their search for bugs. Sparrows hunt for seeds around the barn and in the garden. Geese stay well into December even as the lakes begin to freeze. We have seen robins as late as January, and pine siskins as well as ruby crowned kinglets often stay all winter. The siskins travel in great flocks of 100 or so, swooping across the fields, diving down to alight where there is salt on the ground, picking it up out of the snow, twittering constantly. In a twinkling, as if from a signal, the multitude rises into the air and flies off, only to return a minute later.

Migratory birds sometimes arrive too early and find winter is not really over and they must return to a warmer climate for a few days. If they do this, all is well but one year most of the small birds had come unusually early due to a warm spell at the end of March. On April 11 the temperature fell to 12°F in the morning. The next day we found dead robins and juncos all over the countryside.

A sound we've never succeeded in identifying for certain may come from a lynx. It moves from place to place as though on wings, but emits a screech that is not at all bird-like.

There are other sources of noise, such as loons, eagles, wolves and the familiar "crook-crook" of the raven. But the most cacophonous noise we hear is the anguished shrieking of many of our own gates. Each one has a different voice but all sound as if it were being slowly and cruelly murdered each time it is opened or closed. The drier the weather the louder they squeal. Those with iron pins for hinges are more or less quiet, but most of them have wooden hinges and one of these complains so loudly it can be heard half-way across the farm.

11

Jack and the New Yorkers

The wilderness isn't everyone's natural habitat. Even people who enjoy the outdoors and harbor a longing to spend some time in a totally unspoiled environment sometimes find they are just not suited to it. Much of this is due to having lived in artificial surroundings all their lives, with much of the work being done by other than their personal effort, to the point where this is taken for granted.

Jack tells a marvellously funny story about a man and his son who once engaged him as their guide. They were coming from New York and had arranged to meet Jack where the trail joins the road. The pair were looking forward to spending a week camping at Lonesome Lake. Jack's job was to meet them, bring them to the camp he had set up and then to return them to their car at the end of the week.

What should have been straightforward and uneventful hikes in and out did not turn out precisely that way.

Here is Jack's story.

"I left home at daylight, the 25 miles to the road ordinarily taking about seven hours in summer. There are about 15 miles of trail and 10 miles traversed by boat on the lakes, so I expected to meet the men by noon and have us all back by dark. I got there on schedule, the only delay being a few minutes I spent watching a wolf and a couple of goats on my way.

"The two men, Paul Sr. and his son by the same name

whom I'll call Junior, were just finishing tying on their packs when I arrived. I'd brought along an empty pack board to assist with some of their gear, although they weren't supposed to have anything outside of sleeping bags and personal stuff as I had contracted to supply all required food in the camp. In spite of this, they seemed to have a lot to carry and we each had about 30-pound packs when we started off. I later discovered most of the weight was composed of "necessities" such as canned fruit juice and vegetables.

"Paul explained as we started off that as each member of their family had his or her own car at home, they weren't very accustomed to walking and might not travel very fast. As the day wore on and we averaged about one mile an hour on a good trail, I could see he wasn't fooling.

"Junior had a piece of equipment I'd never seen before—a waist belt with seven snap attachements spaced around it, to which were fastened: a hatchet, a map case, first aid kit, lunch sack, water canteen, a knife and a compass. These swayed rhythmically and jangled musically as we went along, but the belt had added talents. It gradually rotated as he walked so that about once every 15 minutes the axe wound up dangling between his legs. This meant a stop for everyone while Junior removed his pack and by a series of savage jerks, succeeded in twisting the belt back to its original position, from where it immediately began its slow rotation once more.

"He had a Beatle haircut that swayed back and forth in front of his eyes, restricting his vision. Combined with a trail involving upthrust rocks, roots and assorted hazards, together with feet accustomed only to smooth city sidewalks, this impairment resulted in frequent sounds of clattering belt equipment and muttered imprecations as Junior tripped and fell with monotonous regularity.

"After many stops to rest, adjust belt, fall down and pick themselves up, a total of eight miles had been made and we had arrived at the point where the Hotnarko River had to be crossed on a two-foot diameter fir log, 20 feet long and about eight feet above the river. Junior and I had made it over all right but Paul had poor balance, so I dumped my pack and went back for him. After I'd crossed with his pack, he started over. When he reached the middle, he froze and stood there swaying ominously back and forth.

"At this point, Junior shouted, 'Wait there, Dad, I'll help

you.' Not that Dad had much choice. Out went son on the log. When they met in the middle, they stood face to face, holding on to each other's arms, neither of them able to go ahead or to turn around. The impasse was finally solved when Paul moved hesitantly forward while Junior inched backward, the pair of them clinging to each other for dear life. Meanwhile I entertained myself imagining them lying on the rocks below, injured too badly to travel and wondering how in the world I'd ever get them out to the road for medical attention if I had to. I also pondered what we'd do even if they survived this crossing. There was still Lake Creek further ahead which involved walking a slippery 10-inch log across turbulent water. But the gods were kind and they finally traversed Hotnarko safely.

"From there to the first boat took an hour-and-a-half. This part of the trip was enlivened by Paul putting on bursts of speed and getting out of Junior's sight. This impelled Junior to start shouting: 'Dad! Dad! Where are you? Are you all right?' until we overtook him. Junior then somehow got far enough ahead that his father screamed into the forest: 'Paul! Wait for us! Paul! Can you hear me? *You wait for us!*'

"Arriving at the Snag Lake (Stillwater) boat which was rather on the small side for the three of us and our packs (Paul Sr. must have weighed close to 250 pounds), I cautioned them to sit very still in the middle to keep us in balance. We then started up the lake, hauled the boat out a mile-and-a-half up the river from the head of the lake and headed up the three-mile trail to Lonesome.

"We'd gone only half-a-mile when we had to stop and rest again, for the two tenderfeet were pretty tired. Paul and I were sitting on one side of the trail and Junior was on the other side, the bottom of his packboard resting on the top of the log he was relaxing against. I just happened to be looking his way as the packboard slipped off the log and the unexpected jerk of it pulled him over backwards! He landed on his back, on top of the pack, in a depression in the ground just the right size to hold him and his pack in a snug fit.

His legs were over the log and his chin was pressed onto his chest by the fact the back of his head was resting on the edge of the hole.

He was helpless as an upended beetle!

"As he produced muffled and incoherent sounds of

111

protest at his predicament, his father, who hadn't seen what happened, snapped: 'What's wrong, son?' waited a few seconds for an answer and when none was forthcoming, said irritably: 'God damn it—when I ask a question I want an answer!' At this point I went over, helped Junior to his feet and we got underway again, making another half-mile before dark. We had walked a grand total of 11 miles in ten hours.

"As we ate a cold meal in the dark I made the mistake of trying to entertain them by recounting some grizzly tales. They informed me plaintively the next morning they had spent most of the six hours of darkness waiting tensely to be attacked by bears and had jumped every time a leaf rustled.

"We started off at daybreak and they both chose to wade Lake Creek rather than use the log, much to my relief. By 8 a.m. they were finally in the camp and I went on home.

"A week later when I went back to escort them out, I learned they had enjoyed an uneventful week at the camp except for Junior accidentally shooting through a can of syrup when he was target shooting with his .22 pistol.

"With considerably lighter packs, we made better time on the way back and were soon at the Snag Lake boat. When we'd come up earlier I'd landed the boat in a small but swift channel of the river. In order to get out to the main channel it was necessary to start the gear shiftless outboard with the boat headed for a 10-foot-wide gap between an island and a big fir log which sloped off our shore and into the river.

"After we were all loaded, I warned them to sit still in the middle once we got under way down the turbulent river in the heavily laden boat. I asked Paul to hold on to a cedar branch to keep the boat in the correct position while I started the motor. I explained I would tell him when to let go.

"He seemed to understand, so I pulled on the starting cord. The motor caught momentarily. Paul instantly let go of the branch, just as the engine quit. In far too short a time for me to grab an oar to fend us off, we were swept down the six feet of fast water to crunch against the knotty log with a lot of force.

"In five minutes I'd worked the boat up to where we'd started from. Paul again held the branch, after assuring me he wouldn't let go until I gave him the word.

"I pulled the starting cord again and I'll be damned if it

wasn't a repeat of the first time. The motor caught briefly, he let go, the motor died.

"Crunch...again!

"I'd back-packed the 4 x 12 sheets of plywood up from the road ten miles away to build this boat and as I didn't want to have to repeat that performance, I began to get a little exasperated.

"When we were once more at the starting position, I informed Paul if he let go of the branch this time before I told him to, he could walk down the trail around the lake, while I took the boat down alone!

"This time all went smoothly. The motor started and after letting it run at slow speed for a minute, I told Paul to release the branch and we shot straight through the gap to the river beyond.

"When we started downstream I was in the stern seat facing forward with the outboard steering handle projecting past my left side. Paul was in the middle seat facing the stern. In the section between the middle seat and the bow were the three packs stacked so that a narrow aisle down the center allowed access and finally, on the bow deck, also facing aft, was Junior.

"We'd gone only about 200 yards downstream at a combined motor and current speed of perhaps 15 miles an hour when suddenly Paul flung himself over to the right side of the boat, pointed up at a tree top and exulted, 'Look at that eagle!' at which Junior also leaned far right. With their combined weight tipping the boat, the gunwale dipped and water began pouring in.

"As soon as I realized what was happening, I heaved myself to the left in an effort to level the boat. In doing so, I hit the outboard steering handle and pushed it over to the extreme left. This, of course, threw the boat into a 90 degree turn to the right so we headed straight for the bank, full speed.

"Since they were facing astern, and as everything happened so rapidly, neither of the two men knew what was about to happen and were quite unprepared for the sudden stop when we hit the bank. Luckily it was of soft sand at that point. We struck the shore and I got the motor turned off just as Paul went flying backwards off his seat, landing wedged on his back between the packs. Junior flew backwards over the bow and landed on his back on the sand bar, his legs still up on the deck!

"Five minutes later we were organized once more. I'd inspected the bow for damage for we had bumped an old log embedded in the sand when we hit. The two men were reloaded and given a stern warning that if they didn't sit still for the remainder of the trip, they'd be put ashore to walk the rugged five miles around the lake. We made the run to the far shore without further incident.

"By early afternoon we were within a couple of miles of their car and despite advice to the contrary, Junior insisted on going ahead of us and was soon out of sight. I was carrying a rifle on the odd chance of any trouble with grizzlies over trail rights. In the area we were going through there had been a big pale sow with two yearling cubs in residence for the past four months. She had contested the trail with two people already.

"Ten minutes after Junior had vanished off ahead, we were passing a dense patch of red willow with a small, dry watercourse running parallel to the trail about 10 feet from it. I was startled by a sudden loud grizzly grumble in the gully, followed instantly by a great crashing as the bear smashed through the willow towards us. I went at once to the far side of the trail to allow time to sight and to shoot if necessary as she crossed the trail. I assumed Paul would be right behind me, but when I got into position I looked around and couldn't see him.

"Then I spotted him, on the bear's side of the trail, his head shoved into the willows, peering towards the noise of smashing branches, snorts and growls and asking cheerfully: 'Is that a deer?'

" 'No, that's a very angry bear, and you'd better get behind me, *right now*', I said grimly. When the meaning of this sank in, he made record time crossing the trail just as the sow got to the edge of it and grumbled there a few minutes. She then took her cubs off, muttering in an irritated fashion as they headed for the river. When she was well away we continued and reached the car just as Junior was starting to turn it around.

"The road at this point had been bulldozed out of big slide rocks and was walled on both sides by boulders three or four feet high. Where the car (a new one with only 1400 miles on it) was being turned, the road between the rocks was only

114

about four feet wider than the length of the car. When we arrived, young Paul had just manoeuvred the vehicle crosswise.

"His father at once took command. 'O.K. Paul, I'll tell you when to stop before you hit that boulder.'

" 'All right, Dad.'

"Crash! The car shot ahead and smashed into the rocks. With an unhappy grimace, Paul Sr. shouted: 'Not so fast, Paul. Go slow and stop when I tell you to.''

" 'O.K., Dad.'

"Smash! The car darted back and hit the rock embankment. Paul Sr. danced an excited little jig and roared. 'Damn it, Paul! Don't go so *fast*. Just let her creep and stop when I tell you. Now go ahead . . . *easy.*'

" 'All right, Dad.'

"Bash! Again the car leaped ahead and bounced off the boulder in front. In a pained voice, the older man admonished his son. 'You won't go slow enough. I'd better do it. You haven't driven enough to get out of a place like this. Let me have it.'

"Junior got out and his father climbed in. 'Now watch this, son, and see how it's done', he said as he closed the door. The car moved slowly back until about a foot from the rock. Then suddenly jerking the last few inches—crash! Junior turned away. He didn't think it wise to let his father see the grin he couldn't suppress. Paul Sr. viciously turned the wheel as far to the right as it could be forced and yawed onto the road, misjudging the distance and scraping the left front fender as he did so. The car was on the road, headed in the right direction, at last.

"Goodbyes were said and as I turned thankfully to head home, I heard a long screech. It was the oil pan dragging over a high rock in the middle of the road as they rounded a bend and disappeared from sight!''

12

Bathing Bears and Growling Grizzlies

Grizzly bears are reported to be retiring beasts which tend to keep away from the habitations of man. The one I will tell you about doesn't fit that description.

This large silvertip was having a bath only 30 feet behind my cabin. I had been working on a shed until dusk and had just arrived home when I heard splashing noises coming from Bear Bath, my water hole. I walked around to the end of the cabin to see what was making the sound and discovered the silvertip there. He was having a great time sprawling in the bath then lurching out, streaming muddy water, to shake himself. His long fur threw spray 10 feet in all directions. Then he'd rub his back on the nearby trees, turn around and wallow back into the water again. He must have seen or smelled me eventually for he jumped out of his bath, stood on his hind legs a moment, then went rolling across the clearing to the river about 150 feet away. I was disappointed he left in such a hurry as I had never had the chance to observe a bathing bear before!

In case the reader doesn't know it, a "bear bath" is a place where a small stream has dug a deep pool out of soft mud and it is generally four or five feet across. There are often spruces and cedar trees bearing claw and tooth marks surrounding the bath. The bears like to rub their backs on these rough trees, then tromp off leaving huge, deep dents in the mossy wet ground.

117

One bear we met on the trail earned the nickname "plywood bear" because it was intimidated by the plywood intended for Phalarope, the Lonesome Lake boat. The packing job was nearly finished and we were working hard to get the stuff from Stillwater to Lonesome Lake with two horses. I was leading them and carrying two-year-old Susan on my back in a special chair. Jack was in the lead with a slab of 14 x 2 fir plywood tied on each side of his packboard and roped together at each end, creating a box around him. He could only see straight ahead. As Jack went around a bend in the trail, an angry mama grizzly came lumbering across a small stream and to within 15 feet of the pack outfit. We all stopped abruptly and Jack swung the plywood around so he could see what was happening. As soon as he did that, the bear slid to a halt, tumbled over backwards and landed on the run, putting as much distance between herself and that apparition as she could! She went splashing across the creek, almost obscuring herself in spray, gathered her cubs and went huffing off into the dense undergrowth much faster than she had come over in the first place.

A few days later during supper in camp, little Susan kept repeating over and over the amusing words, "Bear plashing more water." We couldn't make out what she was saying for awhile but finally caught on she was talking about that splashy old mama bear.

Some bears are big and obnoxious but we met one which was tiny but plenty obnoxious just the same. We were returning from taking the horses to their fall range and as we were coming across the field in front of the house, were met by the smallest two-year-old grizzly I've ever seen. She wasn't even as large as an ordinary black bear but still had the temerity to question our right to continue the last 150 feet to our house. Not that she charged, or anything as aggressive as that, she simply refused to get out of our way and allow us to proceed. We didn't want to kill the bear so we shouted at her. She kept coming closer so I told our dog Skye to get her out of our way. The bruin stood and watched the barking, jumping, growling dog as if Skye were merely some insignificant little toy. The dog decided she couldn't budge the bear by noise and certainly wasn't going to tackle it, so she returned to us. We advanced to a position close enough for any but the stupidest bear to recognize as time to head out. Still she advanced and since we had a young calf on a picket chain and a small daughter who would not take kindly to being confined to the house, we somewhat reluctantly decided we couldn't risk the bear hanging around, so it would have to be eliminated.

After this unpleasant job was completed, we skinned the beast and nailed its hide to the barn wall to dry. To our surprise, on returning from a trip a short time later, we discovered that another bear had come and ripped the skin off the wall and carried it away. We never found it.

The meat of this bear looked and smelled quite pleasant so we tried cooking a bit of it and found it palatable as hamburger, or rather bearburger, after every scrap of fat was removed. The meat had to be eaten hot or it developed a decidedly fishy taste.

Another bear encounter featured a huge creature, old enough to know better but which decided to contest our right of way. That was not at all funny.

On the morning of May 19, 1965, Jack crept out of bed, dressed quietly, took his rifle and a small hand axe and left the house without waking Susan. He was going up to erect a fence near Tenas Lake to keep the milk cow from going south to join the rest of the herd. I stayed in bed but was awake, so clearly heard the shot which rang out some time later. I figured from the elapsed time that Jack had gone about half-way to Tenas Lake and presumed he had seen a cougar and shot it. That was the main reason he bothered with the rifle.

Jack returned shortly, smelling of bear. "I thought I asked you not to shoot any bears," I complained, as I dislike the job of fleshing them.

"I had to kill this one, or be knocked over," he replied.

He was going along the trail, thinking of something besides bears. He had his Winchester 30-30 slung over his shoulder by a piece of strong nylon rope. In his right hand was his trail axe. All of a sudden he caught sight of an immense brown shape about 40 feet away. His eyes jerked up and met the gaze of the bear. Instantly, old bruin started down the trail toward Jack at a full rolling gallop. While lifting the rifle he raised the peep sight and levered a bullet into the chamber. All this took only a second or two but the bear was closing at great speed. It was just three feet beyond the muzzle of the gun when Jack sighted on the middle of its massive head and squeezed the trigger. The huge creature fell in his tracks, practically at Jack's feet. The bear hadn't even taken time to growl but just before he was shot he opened his cavernous mouth and showed all his teeth. Lying on the ground, he seemed to cover an awful lot of territory. Jack decided the skinning would be easier with help, so he returned home.

We had breakfast, then all of us, with Skye, went up. When Skye smelled the bear scent on Jack she became very interested. When we were a few hundred feet from the bear she grew so excited she could hardly keep still. Heeling as she had been trained to do, she was last in line and when she saw the bear her hackles went up, she growled savagely and barked loudly. Skye leaned forward, keeping her feet as far from the bear as possible as she sniffed at the fallen monster. She undoubtedly knew it was dead, but was taking no chances. When we moved it to start skinning, she growled even more.

His great brown bulk looked larger than a big steer. His head was 20 inches from occiput to his big square nose and almost a foot wide under his tattered ears. We skinned him because we don't like to waste anything, although his hide was poor quality. We later measured the hide and found it to be eight-feet-nine-inches long and seven-feet-four-inches wide across the hind paws. Jack's bullet had entered the bear's head a little above and between the eyes and blasted the whole right side of his brain. No wonder he dropped and never moved again. His hide with the four paws on weighed about 80 pounds. After we had stretched the hide to dry and cleaned the skull up, we began to see this was a pretty big bear. Jack wrote to The University of British Columbia asking what sort of bear we had. Dr. Ian McTaggart-Cowan replied it was a grizzly all right and very likely a new world's record. He asked permission to measure the skull so we sent it down. He sent the information to the Boone and Crockett Club. It was confirmed as the World's record grizzly at that time.

Cubs can be quite playful at times. While packing in the swan feed one October we were just about half-way down one of the grades when we noticed some grizzly bears directly below us in the river. There was a female and her three yearlings. As the river at this point is quite noisy and we were a couple of hundred feet up the rockslide, they were unaware of us and we were able to observe their antics. Two of the cubs were pushing each other around in the waist-deep water. Meantime, mama bear wandered off downstream in her ceaseless search for humpback salmon. Another cub came out from under the bank, climbed up on it, then sort of fell and slid back into the water. The two boxing bears became so serious in their play they both reared up to full height, put their paws on each other's shoulders and pushed mightily, each one endeavoring to clamp his jaws on the other's throat. At last one gave a little harder shove than the other and sent his opponent over on his back in the roiled up water.

We have not yet had any trouble with bears getting into our highly vulnerable freight piles but one miniature grizzly decided to play with the dog for a bit, apparently all in fun.

We had brought the five horses carrying 1200 pounds of swan feed up from Atnarko to the north end of Stillwater, unpacked them and rafted them across the river. On the return from the second trip with horses Susan cooked the lunch while Jack and I began to load 6,500 pounds of grain on the Mary P. Lunch was ready in 15 minutes or so and as we were very hungry, we stopped loading and ate. After the meal we returned to the loading job, leaving Susan to clean up the "kitchen".

Jack and I had just taken a sack of grain each onto the raft and were resting for a second before going back for more when I heard a faint rustling sound like something walking slowly through the long slough grass which grows along the base of the rockslide. I turned and whispered to Jack that there was a bear nearby. The grizzly was so small it was almost hidden by the grass as it poked around in the holes between the boulders at the base of the slide, moving towards us along the shore. A rope we used to assist in turning the raft was tied to a small alder and when the bear came to that it turned, walked over to the rope and sniffed it all over. Meanwhile, Susan had come aboard the Mary P. so we all stood and watched. When the bear was sniffing the rope, I reached out and grabbed it where it was tied to the raft and jerked it so it jumped up in front of the bear. He cocked his head on one side and sniffed some more. The bear was only about 25 feet from us across the shallow, stump-filled bay where the raft was moored. Skye was up on the hill, upwind of the bear, as yet unaware of its presence. As the bear certainly knew we were there and was apparently not alarmed, we began to speak aloud. Finally as the bear continued on his way, we started to shout at it since we had begun to wonder what would happen if he came to the open butter and jam jars in the "kitchen" and we wanted to induce him to decamp up the slide before we found out!

The only result of our shouting was to rouse the sleeping border collie who immediately leapt to her feet and went raging toward the grizzly. At first the bear started up the slide, but after loping over only a few boulders, seemed to decide he wasn't about to expend all that energy for the sake of a 40-pound dog bellowing at his heels, so he whirled and began to chase the dog. Pursued by the grizzly, Skye headed for the raft. As we certainly didn't need a terrified dog plus a clumsy bear on board, I yelled at her, "Get out, get out!" Altogether there was considerable noise. I was shouting at Skye who was barking frantically as she ran in front of the annoyed bear and Jack was shouting at the bear! The dog didn't come onto the raft but she led the bear all around the freight piles, past the open food and back again. Eventually the grizzly decided he'd had enough exercise so left the scene and plunged into the river with a splash. He was soon on the other side. Surprisingly, all those clawed feet failed to rip even a single hole in any of the plastic covers lying about on the ground where the bear and dog had their game of tag.

We have been very lucky so far as we have sustained little damage by bears. One threw a five-gallon fuel tank off the raft and chewed up the fuel hose. Another one punched three or four holes in a quart can of power saw gas we had left hidden in the woods from a trail-clearing operation. When the gas spilled, the bear rolled on the gas-soaked ground. For some reason bears seem to like gas and oil and even roll and rub themselves in oily power saw dust.

13

Furred and Feathered Neighbors

The trumpeter swans afford us much pleasure in observing them each day because, although the job of feeding and reporting on them is officially in my name, the whole family shares in both the work and the enjoyment involved in caring for the huge birds.

As we walk down on Big Lagoon a number of birds get impatient, take off from the feedplace and fly up, circling the person coming to feed them and trumpeting all the way as they fly back. Sometimes a bunch of them come walking up the ice to meet us. They advance a short distance, then sit down on the ice, tuck their big webbed feet up under their wings and thick feathers to warm them and, after a few minutes, will rise and walk some more. They keep doing this until they reach us. After we pass they all turn and start the slow march back, with stops to warm their feet.

When winter is more than half-done, and sometimes earlier, the swans commence to fight and court one another. There is a lot of noise or singing and whooping as they chase one another around. Some warm days they will chase and court as much as they eat. Then they get out on the ice and preen themselves. In courtship two adult swans of opposite sex face each other and bob their heads up and down while raising their wings to half mast, then fluttering them, all the time gabbling and whooping. When they begin, their heads are high as they can be held. As they duck them down, either in unison or alternately, their heads are lowered right down until the bills almost rest on their breasts, then up go the heads as high as possible again. When the heads are down the long sinuous necks describe an almost perfect, nearly closed letter C. Their trumpetings can be heard over a distance of a couple of miles on a clear day.

Occasionally on a cold moonlit night when the timber is cracking and the ice booms, all the adults in the flock get together and stage a concert. It is the most thrilling thing I have ever heard, aside from a pack of wolves in chorus. The wolves are spine-tingling while the trumpeter music is majestic and harmonious. The cygnets keep quiet while the adults sing as their voices are not fully developed until they are at least 18 months old. The trumpeters' calls are very difficult to describe. Although I have heard them thousands of times, I cannot think of words to describe adequately the various calls they can produce. The tone, timbre and quality of their trumpeting is more sonorous than a trumpet. The bird's windpipe winds around through his sternum and bends sharply up over a ridge of bone to form a loop before continuing to his lungs. The more common whistling swan does not have this loop and his voice is sort of a soft squeak. It is therefore believed the extra loop is responsible for the quality and volume of the trumpeter's call.

They have several different calls which seem to express varying ideas. The landing call, very distinct, is composed of two high notes followed by two lower notes, then two more high ones and a low one. This call signals their intention to land. If there are already some swans down, those on the water will reply with a single short note. The landing call may be a question to those already down, asking if it is safe to land. Whenever something frightens the flock, one of them will stand, head held high as possible, and sound the alarm. This is a strident, urgent, stacatto note, repeated at frequent intervals. If the threat is serious, more of them will take up the alarm, nervously bobbing heads a short distance up and down. If nothing bothers them further the sounds gradually subside and they go back to the "at ease" trumpeting, courting and wing-flapping. If the threat continues to menace, more and more of the flock take up the call and it becomes a babble of sharp, strident notes sounding closer and closer together until it is almost a roar. At that point the entire flock of up to 400 birds somehow launches itself into the air after a brief scrambling take-off. The alarm gradually gives way to the musical "at ease" signal as the big birds get further and further away from the threat. They trumpet softly with all the short, low notes produced smoothly. A male produces higher notes standing high as he can. These convey to me a' happy exuberance and love of life seldom heard from any other bird. I don't know if there is any difference in the voices of males and females but it generally seems to be a large-necked swan that trumpets the loudest notes. It is not easy to identify individuals. The alarm call conveys desperate fear but all other calls ranging from the low, happy semi-grunts of a swan with its bill full of grain and water to the rapid gabbling of a courting or fighting group seem to express a sense of pure, wild joy.

Occasionally someone accidentally frightens the birds by dropping the feed dish or breaking off a large section of shore ice when they don't expect it. Then the feeding flock will instantly plunge to the far side of the pool amidst a tremendous spray of water, churning feet and flailing seven-foot wings! They swarm out on the ice until with perhaps 20 feet between them and the feeder, they feel safe. They then stand tall, flap their wings vigorously, shake like feathered dogs and whoop loudly for five minutes or so. After congratulating themselves on having escaped the attacking feed dish, they all begin sliding back into the pool and start picking up grain as if nothing had happened.

It takes the swans only about 20 minutes to clean up their meal, no matter how many are present. Ten swans get only five pounds of food and 200 pounds of grain feeds double that number of swans. The ones closest to the person feeding get the most and are done first. These are generally the cygnets. The adults rarely shove them aside, apparently recognizing their need to be greater since they are less hardy than the old birds. When eating off the ice they take longer to retrieve all the grain.

As more and more swans finish eating, they scramble out on the ice at the far side of the pool. This can be quite a procedure with the swans sliding back into the water several times before resorting to wing power to help them onto the slippery surface. They swim up to the edge, slide their breasts up onto it as far as possible, then by extending their long necks straight in front as counterweights, weave to and

125

fro as they gradually work themselves onto the ice. At last they get the middle claw of one foot on and if that doesn't slip off, the swans can lever themselves out onto the surface of the ice. Once out, they stand up, look around importantly, then sit down. If it is cold, they bury their feet in their feathers.

Frequently they begin preening themselves, standing and lifting first one wing and then the other to hunt all around through their feathers for the large, light brown lice that seem to parasitize all swans. After completing this operation the swan lays his head over his back and rubs his bill on the "oil nozzle" at the base of his tail. Then he brings his oily bill forward and proceeds to oil his feathers, starting on the lower part of his neck and working back. He must return to the nozzle many times before the job of anointing himself has been completed satisfactorily. The part of the body oiled last is the head, accomplished by turning the head over and rubbing the top of it on the oil nozzle. There is very little noise while all the preening is going on, just the odd croak and an occasional single high note with a questioning inflection. At times the preening is done on the water. More often than not a swan becomes so engrossed in the job he stops moving his feet to hold position in the slow current and will drift down the pool like a chunk of foam. Grooming completed, the swan opens his wings, flaps vigorously, then sits down, tucks his feet into those cozy feathers, rests his head along his back, shoves his bill under a wing and goes to sleep. Oddly enough, they always seem to put their heads under the left wing.

In warm weather a swan will sleep fitfully with the top of his bill just under the wing while his head remains up where he can see by opening just one eye. I don't believe much could sneak up on them while they sleep. Often they stand quietly on the ice on one leg, the other stretched out far behind, their heads under their wings.

Swans on the water ordinarily float buoyantly but they are capable of sinking so low they almost submerge. They do this to hide from enemies or in preparation for launching an attack on another swan and sometimes merely to wash ice from their feathers and wings. In the last operation the swan will sink low, then heave its breast out of the water, suddenly plopping down on the surface to create a wave. The manoeuvre is repeated until all the ice has been melted by the water washing over it. They use their bills to assist the ice removal if the water treatment proves inadequate, grabbing chunks of ice and pulling gently until it slides from the wing or tail feather. They must de-ice themselves or they will be too heavy to fly. The ice spoils the lift as well as creating resistance to the airflow. Ice forms on them any time temperatures are below zero.

While the swans can sink deep into the water they are also able to rise high out of it to shake themselves or to flap their wings. By treading water they can rise so high as to appear to be standing on the surface for a few seconds.

Trumpeter swans usually hold their necks straight up although some of them hold their necks in the "S" shape as mute swans do. The trumpeters, however, practically never elevate the aft ends of their wings, either while floating or standing.

Sometime during the afternoon, after the swans have finished preening and napping, the flock begins to break up. Families and small groups fly off, up or down the valley to dig for more feed in any open places they can find. A good number of them seem to spend the night at Stillwater, about 10 miles distant. They return in groups in the morning after the sun rises. Trumpeters seem to fly mostly during daylight hours, although they are quite capable of flying when it is dark. They often arrive at the feedplace with both feet hidden in their feathers, though when it is warm, the feet lie stretched close under the tail.

While feeding the swans each day, we have the chance to observe a variety of wild animals and birds. Several years back while I was watching the swans eat, a goldeneye duck flew into the midst of the 100 or more trumpeters and half a dozen mallard ducks. The goldeneye is a diving duck while the mallard is supposed to be a surface feeder. The little goldeneye wanted the mallard to move so he could have the grain the mallard was stealing from the swans but since the intruder was much smaller, he used stealth to get his way. He would line up on the mallard, dive under the water, swim to where the mallard was feeding, then pop up right under the bigger duck, causing it to depart hurriedly to a different part of the feedhole while the goldeneye ate the grain. He would then proceed to do the same thing to another mallard. The tiny duck must have spent as much time chasing as it did eating!

We find wolves interesting. One winter while I was still living at my parents' home, there were several timber wolves up on the hillside. I learned to mimic them so well I had them running from side to side of the valley trying to locate me. One day I had been teasing them for about an hour in the morning before starting out to feed the swans. The wolves were quiet as I set off for the "swannery". I used the trail around Big Lagoon as the ice was covered with deep snow and a lot of springs had made holes all over the ice. I was walking along through the soft snow when something caused me to stop and look to my left. No more than 20 feet away, and standing broadside, were three of the handsomest wolves I have ever seen. One was light gray with rusty-brown legs and a beautiful white collar of long fur around the neck. The others were shiny black. Only a few skinny lodgepole pines separated us. As soon as I stopped and turned in their direction, dropping my pack of grain, they all exchanged ends and fled up the hill, vanishing in a flash. I had expected trouble from them and as I was unarmed, had dropped my pack to be better able to climb a tree. They obviously didn't want to eat me and weren't even uncomfortable about my approach. I believe they were only curious as to what sort of creature could make a noise so like them yet bear no resemblance. I know of two other instances where wolves have followed or come to people and showed no aggressiveness.

In 1960 Jack was walking along the ice on Lonesome Lake before daybreak. As he was proceeding parallel to the shore, he heard noises like dogs whining which kept up as he went along. Several wolves were going along abreast of him. He couldn't see them because it was not yet light, but on his way home in the afternoon he discovered a half-mile or so of their tracks travelling just inside the timber along the lake shore. Just before he reached the tracks he spotted eight wolves sprawled on the ice, resting after feasting on a deer they had killed. He could see them from a slight rise although they were clear across the lake, about three-quarters of a mile away. As he wanted to reduce the bunch a little and could not go over the thin ice they were on, he howled and whined until he got a reply. After they conversed awhile in this manner, the wolves decided to come and investigate. Jack crept down to the lake shore without letting the wolves see him. On hands and knees he descended about 500 feet as the wolves approached, whining and wagging their tails. By the time Jack reached bottom, the wolves were only 100 feet off shore. They wouldn't come closer, so Jack picked one good target and shot it. The others swept back across the lake, somewhat wiser and probably sadder. The reason for killing any wolves is that when there are too many in this area they pose a threat to domestic stock so we prefer they should not become too numerous. We enjoy hearing them and don't want to eliminate the species by any means.

The second time Jack called wolves he had no intention of killing any. They were just across the river and Jack wanted some pictures of them. I stayed at the house and howled at them while Jack went over where they were. There were tracks everywhere and when I howled, I got a reply. The snow was soft so Jack was able to get close and when he gave a single whine, the woods magically filled with wolves. There were gray ones and blacks, running and whining, coming from all directions to within 15 feet or so of where Jack stood under a dense fir tree. They could not see him and ran around in circles, sniffing and conversing with one another. One, behind a large log, would stand up and put its paws on the log, look around a few seconds and drop down behind the log again. It repeated the performance a number of times while Jack communicated with the group. One wolf got a stick and began to play with it like a dog. It was unfortunate it was so dark in the woods, for Jack was unable to get any good pictures.

These wolves obviously were not aggressive as there were 13 of them in the band and they could easily have pulled him down if they chose. Eventually Jack showed himself and the wolves took off in all directions at great speed. In retreating, one of them jumped a distance of 15 feet horizontally and six feet vertically to land on top of a small bluff. They ran so fast they appeared almost to fly. I believe many people have unjustified prejudice against wolves which they would lose if they looked on them merely as creatures living in the manner they were intended to and not as blood-thirsty demons out to slaughter indiscriminately. Sometimes wolves are just plain curious.

Otters are also fascinating to watch. On one trip to the horse range, Jack was walking along the shore of Tenas Lake when he saw an otter on the ice near a spring hole. It stopped what it was doing and looked at him. Since the otter seemed so attentive, Jack made a snowball and rolled it across the ice in the otter's direction. The little creature caught it and chomped it up. Jack threw him another and the otter caught that too. After playing with the otter for awhile, Jack continued on his way.

Another time Jack passed the same spot and watched two otters playing. As one lay on its back, the other would come humping along and leap onto the paws of the upside-down otter which promptly ousted the "attacker", who then galloped off to repeat the procedure.

On one of the swan-feeding trips, Jack saw an otter on the river near the Edwards' place. As he enjoys these animals, he stopped to see what it would do. She came out from under the ice and onto a large log on which there was snow and ice. She piled the snow and kept patting it down and piling more until she had it exactly to her specifications. Then she sat over it and passed her excrement on top of the snow pile, a look of pure bliss on her face! After this performance, she slid around on the ice and snow, finally rolling over on her back, draping her thick tail up over her belly as she batted it to and fro with her front paws. The tail was twitching back and forth as though trying to evade the paws.

We derive pleasure, too, from the plucky little water ouzel who sings his cheerful song as he swims around in water filled with chunks of ice. While timber cracks like rifle fire and the sky is a cloudless blue, the water ouzel acts as if he doesn't even know it is cold. In fact, the colder it gets, the more cheerful this little bird appears.

Some animals become quite tame when they are not bothered and are supplied with free food. Moose sometimes winter in the valley although there used to be more of them than there are now. The first winter I worked at Fogswamp two or three of them were living on the trees I had felled. Leaving my cabin one cold January day I headed across the small slashing out by the river, wondering if my moose visitor would run away as ooon as he saw me, as usual. Just as he had been for the past week, the moose was nibbling the ends off the topmost branches of a birch tree I had cut down the day before and this time allowed me to come quite close. Standing on an old log, my saw over my left shoulder and the axe in my right hand, I quietly watched him hauling the branches into his grotesque mouth with its overgrown upper lip. After a few moments of nature study I stepped down and started towards a birch tree I wished to fall, wondering how soon the moose would take flight, as my course led me towards him. Seconds after I stepped off the log, that cantankerous old moose stopped eating, lowered his ugly head, flattened his ears onto his neck and rushed towards me at great speed, using his long, reaching stride. Somewhat suprised, I dropped the saw and with my three-pound axe held with both hands high over my head, rushed towards him. If he had continued, my axe would have split his skull for I brought it down with all my might! Fortunately for that ill-tempered beast, he jammed his feet into the ground and lowered his head still further so that his huge nose bumped an old fallen tree at the precise instant my axe sank its blade into the same log!

Recovering his wits, the moose wheeled and trotted off across the clearing with me in hot pursuit, still brandishing my axe and roaring obscenities at his rapidly retreating form! I assume he must have considered the birches his private property and thought he was protecting his food supply, not realizing I had brought the trees to the ground where he could get at them in the first place. His antlers had been shed previously but any animal standing six or seven feet at the shoulders and weighing possibly 1,000 pounds, is no beast to argue with.

Later on in the winter while I was cutting trees, I heard a lot of grunting and crashing of small trees about 100 feet away. It was another moose, bigger than the one I had chased. It was racing around a small clearing, smashing over little trees, tearing up the sand with its hooves and generally acting as if it had gone completely mad. Having learned my lesson, I jumped on my old mare and ran that lumbering creature across the river, down the other bank and back across the river at which time it suddenly decided to vacate the entire area and took off up the mountain! I went back to land-clearing and heard nothing more. I don't know what all the excitement was about unless it was a case of over-whelming joy that the hard winter was nearly over.

When the snow is so deep deer can't get feed easily, we cut trees for them. Even if we aren't cutting trees for their special benefit they always come to where we are clearing land or falling trees for fuel. They get so tame some of them will eat the branch ends off even while the power saw is cutting blocks off the other end. They have actually learned to come to the snarl of the saw when they hear it. I have seen as many as 20 of them eating and trampling the area down with their sharp little hooves.

There is considerable variation in the size of bucks' antlers but I bet one I bagged is something of a record for size. It was way back when I was first working on my place and I saw what appeared to be a doe with a distinctly "bucky" look about it. As I was out of meat, I spent some time trying to get close enough to see if the deer was a buck with short antlers or an antlered doe. I followed as the animal grazed and browsed on my clearing, then sat on a log to wait while it lay down to chew cud. Finally he got up, turned stern to and showed me all I needed for identification! I had him in a few short minutes after that long "stalk". He was indeed, a nice, fat buck. But what ridiculous antlers! Fully two inches long and with very sharp points. What an awful sissy he must have felt!

In our area there are so many wild creatures we are often able to notice unusual things. Many years ago I was walking through the woods one May day when I stumbled over a female ruffed grouse on her nest. She flew off, leaving her 12 speckled eggs exposed. Several days later I was again in the area and noticed a small stream of water had risen right under her nest. As the grouse took off and left her eggs, I looked to see if they were cold. They were, so I raised the nest and drained the water off in channels around both sides. After that I checked the grouse every day and dug out the ditches as the spring melting of snow caused the water to rise. It got so I was able to carry out my regular inspection of the nest one day without the mother even moving as I dug ditches with a hoe right beside her. On my return next day, Mother grouse and eleven of her eggs were gone. She hatched all but one. I figure she would have lost all of them if the water had come up over the nest.

Of the three cat species in British Columbia the cougar is the largest. Its meat tastes like pork and we enjoy getting the odd one to eat. Being shy and wary, they are not easy animals to come across. I saw a mother and her kitten on the road one summer but when they saw me they were gone so quickly I got only a mere glimpse. However, if a kill can be found and a person is persistent, it is possible to see the big, tawny cat.

One spring my mother told us about a cougar kill which

was about half-a-mile north of our place right beside the wagon road. Jack went down early the next morning. He didn't see the cat but could tell it had been back, eaten some more of its deer, then dragged the carcass farther back from the trail and covered it with leaves and sticks. Jack returned several times during the day but didn't see the cat. Next morning the same thing. The cat had come, eaten breakfast, moved the deer, buried it and gone. On the third day as he was cautiously approaching, he spotted the cougar engaged in covering the kill for the day. Jack could not shoot it as it was moving around too much, pawing up dirt and trying to make the deer remains invisible. Jack stopped when he saw the cat and stayed there two hours, waiting for a shot. After the cat got the deer covered, it jumped over a large pine log and lay down with only ears and eyes above the log. After a little while the cougar sprang over the log, grabbed the deer and moved it closer to the log. Then back over the log it sailed, resuming its former position, watching and waiting. During the next hour-and-a-half the cat glided twice over the log, adjusted the deer and vanished. It always moved so quickly and kept so low Jack had no chance to shoot. Brush and trees obstructed his view of everything but the cat's ears and the top of its round head. On its last moving, the cougar ate a little but was clearly ill at ease.

The cougar was unable to see Jack simply because he never stirred while the cat was in a position to see him. Had he moved even a hand, the cat would have caught the movement and fled. As Jack stood and watched his prey, the cat lay on its belly, staring constantly in all directions. Finally, a raven unwittingly rescued Jack from his cramped vigil. It landed on a stick right behind the cat's head. Instantly the cat sprang up, turned towards the intruder and exposed its body just long enough for Jack to shoot it.

He brought the carcass home and skinned her. We were surprised to find relatively little meat in her stomach as the deer had been disappearing at a colossal rate. We didn't solve the mystery then, but got a possible answer a little more than two weeks later on an exciting day which began in quite an ordinary manner.

Even though I am married and don't have to work outside with axes and things, I still do, because it keeps me in condition so that I can work beside my husband if I choose. Quite often Jack does the cleaning and cooking. This suits us and is good for us because we believe in sharing the pleasant jobs as well as the unpleasant ones. At any rate, I was out working one day while Susan and Jack were preparing lunch. I planned to fix some fence and a creek crossing before returning in an hour for lunch. I had only been gone about half-an-hour when I heard a shot. As I wanted to finish what I was doing, I kept working until I heard Jack calling. Then I started for home.

I met him hurrying up to get me and searching for a young calf we had secured on a chain near the barn. I had seen the calf earlier and wondered why she had broken her collar. She had seemed frightened and tried to follow me through the fence, but I didn't suspect what had happened to make her act that way.

Jack quickly informed me he had shot a cougar in the barn, that Susan was locked in the henhouse and that since the one he had shot was small, he feared Ma cougar might be near as well.

I was able to tell him where the calf was and we speedily returned to the barn. After letting Susan out of the henhouse, we got Skye out from behind the woodshed and went looking for more cats. The only scent the dog was able to pick up was where the cougar had come through the fence to ambush the calf. We could not find any sight or trace of more cougars so we collected the calf, brought her back, much against her will, and tied her up on her chain again. As we did so, we noticed a long thin scratch on her face.

What had happened was that soon after I left the house, Susan went to the henhouse to gather eggs. She was just starting to come out when she saw an animal with a hen in its teeth, lying on the ground about 15 feet away. The hens were running around and squawking. One ran into its house past Susan. She slammed the door and yelled to her father. Jack heard the fright in her voice, rushed outside and asked what was wrong. She shouted back there was a lynx, just as he spotted the animal. Susan had never seen a living cougar before but had seen a lynx a few years earlier. The cougar's long tail was hidden from her view. When Jack first saw the cat it was standing up staring around, still with the hen in its mouth, appearing to be trying to decide where to go for dinner. Jack told Susan to stay in the henhouse and to keep the door closed. He then hurried back to the house for his gun, catching a glimpse as he did so of the cat strolling nonchalantly through the barn doorway, 30 feet from the henhouse.

Jack quickly closed the barn door, then placed a ladder against the wall of the hay section, climbed in and slid down to the mangers. With the door closed there was very little light in the barn but as his eyes grew accustomed to the darkness, he briefly glimpsed the white hen move as the cat started its feast and a flash of the cougar's eyes as it lay in the calf manger at the far end of the barn. Jack aimed between the glowing eyes and blasted the cat's head off.

Apparently the cougar had tried to kill the calf but it broke loose and ran away. The cat then came into the henyard, jumped over the three-foot-high wire enclosure and caught the hen.

The killing of this cougar gave us the probable explanation of the other cat's strange behavior and the rapid consumption of her kill. Both cats were almost the same size although the hen killer was extremely thin. They could have been litter mates. The male cougar had broken his leg and it had healed up but he was full of porcupine quills. They were in his mouth, throat and even in his stomach as well as all over his hide. While his hind leg was in the process of healing he would have had a hard time hunting and I suspect the poor beast may have been stealing from the female's kills. She probably tired of his pilfering and had laid a trap for him. He certainly would have been torn to bits if he had been foolish enough to venture close to the female's kill. When Jack dispatched the female, it forced the famished male to hunt for himself. About all he could have managed was the hen.

It was fortunate it was Jack who was home that day because, although I have better than average sight in my left eye, my right is astigmatic and this condition makes an animal appear an indistinct blob through rifle sights. As I never learned to shoot left-handed, I probably wouldn't have been able to hit that cougar in the dark barn.

Perhaps the animal that gives us the most trouble is the bush-tailed pack rat. They come into the house sometimes while we are gone and make a fantastic mess. They have devoured plants, chewed on Susan's toys, damaged some spare saddles and made a stinking nest in the cupboard where we keep our vegetables. The worst damage has been to our freight and horse gear. They will cut anything made of leather or rawhide and what they don't gnaw on they mess up so it stinks and is hardly fit to touch. Aside from that, one will occasionally take a bite out of a human.

One year when we were on our way to start packing, we stopped for the night at our cabin at the south end of Stillwater. During the night we were awakened by some beast rampaging around in our stuff. I shone the flashlight around to see what it was and spotted a huge, gray pack rat sitting on a shelf. I was afraid he might bite little Susan so, since I was on the outside and thoroughly dislike rats anyway, I jumped out of bed in no more than I was born in, grabbed up a small axe and gave chase to the offending creature. The rat jumped off the shelf, ran alongside the top log of the back wall under the roof and right over Susan. He kept dodging first over one side of the rafter and then the other. Every time his head appeared, I took aim with the axe handle and hit him several times but not squarely enough to lay him out. He finally got fed up with my brand of hospitality and in the confusion of his departure, came running up my arm and onto my shoulder. I cussed him and shook him off. He then went scurrying across the floor and disappeared down a crack. This all took only about two minutes, but it seemed forever as that horrid beast ran over my arm.

Next morning I let Skye in the cabin and she immediately started sniffing the crack the rat had gone down. I thought the rodent had left for good but as the dog seemed so sure of herself, I pulled a cleat out of the way and sure enough, that old rat ran out. He had been blinded in one eye and was somewhat befuddled by the battering I had given him. He scuttled out of the cabin, ran to the freight shed and hid between a couple of boxes. We all chased after him and cornered him while I hit him squarely on his stupid noggin, disposing of him in the river.

Smaller animals often give us trouble. One year when we came home, we found our red hens were disappearing. During the night something made one of the two remaining hens squawk dreadfully. We had no decent light so could not stop the marauder which killed her. In the morning we found hen parts strewn around and decided it must have been a weasel, although they don't normally bother our hens.

A few days later we were awakened by a savage growling

136

and snarling upstairs. We ran up and were confronted by an angry marten, one of two which had taken possession of the upper storey and had been fighting over a can of rendered beef fat. Apparently they had decided to spend the winter there and live on our hens. With the aid of the flashlight, Jack shot one. The other escaped but next night we caught it in a trap. It was undoubtedly the martens preying on the hens as a weasel isn't strong enough to drag a whole hen up a four-foot vertical door and through a foot-square ventilator hole.

Sometimes the cats steal our eggs so when we return from a packing trip there are none. While we are home, the cats are caged whenever the hens are laying, being turned loose in the evening to hunt for mice.

One spring quite a lot of broom grass had crowded in close to the main stem of our yellow rose bush in the yard and seedheads were sticking up through the blooming bush. As I was carefully cutting the grass one June day, an angry and alarmed song sparrow burst from the bush and flew to an apple tree where she scolded me for fully five minutes. Her nest with four speckled eggs in it was built in the center of the thorny bush and had been well hidden and shaded by the tall grass. As the sun could now shine directly on her, we compensated for removing the grass by procuring green cedar branches and weaving them into the rose bush. After flying suspiciously around it for a little while, the mother sparrow returned to her nest and settled down on her eggs again.

She had constructed the nest without our knowing a thing about it even though it was right beside the door to the woodshed and we walked past only three feet away several times daily. She must have just started to set when I found her that morning as it was 12 days later before four ugly, nearly naked babies lay huddled in the nest.

After the babies hatched, one parent or the other carried food continuously all through the long June days. The dreadful looking babies grew prodigiously and soon had brown fluff over their scrawny pink bodies. The little creatures' eyes were still closed but their immense yellow beaks gaped wide whenever anything bumped their nest. In about 10 days the nest was heaped with baby birds and the mother was obliged to spread her wings considerably to brood them each night. A few days later their eyes were open

137

and feathers had replaced the fluff. A little later still they were all over the grass and we kept our cats tied until they could fly properly.

Birds and animals don't appear to worry much about human habitation as long as they have some natural surroundings and are not bothered. Even a crow came to our pan of beef renderings put out for whisky jacks and Clark's nutcrackers. Although the crow was hungry, he came only on the coldest days and never became very tame. When he arrived near the fat dish he would sit on a fence post and scrutinize it for a matter of minutes before flying cautiously down in the snow beside the pan. He would then walk over to it, reach his head as far as possible and make a lightning jab at the fat, stab a piece and jump back in a panic. He would then fly away across the field to eat his "catch" in the safety of big trees.

For years we yearned for barn swallows to share our home. Several springs they visited the upstairs of our house but after talking and squabbling for awhile, departed.

When we started work on the addition to our log house and had taken off the gable in the process of joining new to old, the swallows found easier access to the attic. When several of these birds, relatively rare in our area, began to inspect the attic, twittering ecstatically, we hoped they might nest there. For weeks they continued to fly in and out, checking possible sites. They began darting at us as we worked, flying straight at us and turning off only inches away. We could actually feel the wind from their wings as they braked and swerved around us. The work on the addition involved hammering, sawing and running the power saw, yet none of these noises appeared to bother them.

One day we noticed a pair had been daubing small balls of mud along the sheeting. As soon as they stuck one layer on, they plastered on another and some of it would fall off. They finally gave up for a few days. Meanwhile another pair kept flying in through the open windows of the downstairs, daubing their mud haphazardly all over the logs. Much of this fell off, so I made a platform about five inches square and nailed it to the wall. They used it immediately—to rest on! They then placed a row of mud balls in a perfect circle all the way round the board, decided it wouldn't do and went back to plastering the smooth logs again!

On July 6 we discovered the nest of the attic dwellers. The

small, shiny blue birds with their rich bay fronts and long forked tails had been quietly perfecting the little work of art which stood balanced precisely on a brace where there was a ring of knots to help anchor it. Made up of balls of mud patiently prodded into place by the quarter-inch beak, wisps of dead grass acting as binding material, the whole cup-shaped structure was about five inches in diameter. Fine grass and soft white chicken feathers finished it off. Lying in it were four pale, speckled half-inch eggs.

With the attic pair as examples, the downstairs couple now began more purposeful work. One of them, probably the female, starting building the mud and grass in one place, although the other still placed his on the log a foot or so distant. Eventually they agreed on a spot and the structure expanded rapidly. Each morning and afternoon they would work with frenzy, taking turns. As the day wore on the male would quit hauling building materials and instead would take up his position on the post, tiny claws clutching the corner of it, while he sang his encouragement to his hard-working spouse.

The family of the upstairs couple arrived July 13. A day later the downstairs family put the finishing touches on their nest and an egg a day appeared until the female began setting on her clutch of four. Before the actual setting began, we observed how the male would posture, sing and nudge the female who only occasionally answered softly. Once brooding began, the male almost outdid himself with melodic twittering rolling from his throat for seven or eight seconds without a break. At the conclusion, he'd open his beak wide and distend his throat to produce a long vibrant note, essence of joy and pride.

The story had a less than happy ending. Although we made every effort to protect the birds from our two cats, the felines won the battle. This tragedy did not occur until after we had watched the family for a few days. When just tiny, the chicks slept a good deal and the parent would actually have to chirp to awaken them for feeding. They grew rapidly and could soon gape their bills wide when they heard the chirp. Somehow, the parents almost always managed to feed the babies in rotation. By the end of the first week, the chicks had grown so much their heads were as large as the eggs had been, their bodies covered with soft black hair. In two more days dark feathers began sprouting and their eyes started to open. It was then that tragedy struck.

It was obvious the parents were stunned and couldn't believe their nests and babies were gone. The last sight we had of barn swallows that year was a flock which came in the evening, swooping across the sky, twittering and talking for half-and-hour or so. Our hopes that this was a good omen and that they would return the next year and have better luck, were realized. Barn swallows now nest regularly at Fogswamp.

14

Fire!

One hot July day in 1957 we were hunting for our team of horses about half-a-mile north of Fogswamp when we came upon a smouldering piece of dry grass sod. A little breeze was blowing and flames were starting to lick out into dry grass. It would soon have raced through dry leaves to the brush and trees and then off through the woods, a racing, roaring devil of destruction.

We got sand from the river beach, carried it up the bank and smothered the flames. We then rushed home and got a pail and mattock to dig up the soil with, went back and extinguished it completely. The bloody fool who built a fire in the dry sod, instead of down by the water on the sandy beach, had no sense at all.

Another idiot came into this area in mid-summer and camped part way around Lonesome Lake. He also chose to build his fire far from the water, up near some trees. When he left in the morning, he kicked a little dirt over it and went merrily on his way. Several hours later my brother John saw smoke from a mountainside. John and my mother, together with the man who had made the fire in the first place, worked hard to put it out. That fire could have burned us all out and taken a lot of park as well. We were on a horse-buying trip at the time so there weren't many people here to fight fires.

Although the people of the Parks Department appear

sometimes to wish we weren't here, I believe we are not altogether a detriment as we and the Edwards have saved this section of Tweedsmuir Park from certain destruction by fires caused by careless campers.

The park, consisting of about 5,400 square miles, was established in 1936. When the Kenny Dam caused the inundation of a large part of the north end of the park, the boundaries were moved south to compensate for some of the loss. The former southern boundary had been a few miles north of Lonesome Lake. Now the park encompasses both the Edwards' and our place.

There have been other fires in the years since we became part of the provincial park. We have found several camps where people built their fires in dry humus under big fir trees in the hot summer months. I suppose they didn't want to park their tender rumps on hard rocks! Even when they manage to make their fires on beaches they build them on the high side next to the timber instead of at the water's edge where they are easier to extinguish.

In this area it is not safe to burn after the first of April, except at night. The charred remains of the pile will often be smoking the next day. When the almost inevitable wind comes up around 10 in the morning, we carry pails of water and drench the smoldering heap for fear that embers might be blown to dry rotten stumps and take hold.

In the spring of 1955 I did a lot of burning and had thought I'd made certain all the piles were burned out. Unfortunately, some fire remained inside a rotten cedar log. About two weeks later, around the middle of April while I was on a trip to Bella Coola, an extremely hot and drying south wind sprang up. This stirred the embryonic fire into magnificent growth in seconds. When I had set the piles burning in the first place the ground was frozen hard so the fire merely seared the surface needles. When that warm wind stirred the little blaze into life, it galloped gaily over the previously burned-out area a second time. By then the layer of needles next to the ground had dried out. As the fire raged around, seeking things to devour, it sent up a dense cloud of smoke.

My people saw it and hurried the mile-and-a-half to try to stop it but the hot wind had carried the flames across my slashing section to a small shed I had built the first year on the place. They could do nothing to save it. There was a bit

142

of hay and dry horse manure inside which burned readily. The fire then crowned in a fir tree towering over the shed and dropped flaming branches onto the dry shake roof. It burned to the ground. Having lost the shed, my folks then attempted to save my possessions in the cabin by throwing them into the swamp. However, the fire raced northward with the wind and didn't come close to the cabin. After running lightly over a field it rushed at the wall of standing timber, even crowning in the first ranks of green Douglas firs. Because the ground was still wet from the recently melted snow farther back in the forest, the conflagration at last died.

I arrived home the day after the fire got away so was able to help in vanquishing the enemy. When the fire raged through the fir forest it gnawed its way into the pitchy roots of many of the trees and it took a solid week of chopping to extinguish these. We poured bucket after bucket of water into some hollow roots until they over-flowed and killed the embers clinging to the interiors.

This accident proved a good, if costly, lesson and we have been fanatically careful with our burning since that time. We do much of it during the winter months.

As our small clearing is completely surrounded with resinous evergreens, we have a real dread of fire. Although that one did not get off my boundaries, it showed what could happen even when one is being careful.

One night recently we were all sitting around the big yellow table in the kitchen and someone started to tell the Tale of the Helicopter Pilot. In no time everyone got into the act, adding details, teasing me about how mad I had been, tossing caustic comments in regard to the denseness of the helicopter pilot concerned and generally getting a lot of laughs out of recounting the incident.

Susan and I were just emerging from the woods after the three of us had made a trip to the range to pick up some stock. Jack had taken a trail which would bring him home a little ahead of us as we were leading the horses.

Suddenly I smelled smoke. I thought that was darned funny. It was the first of June and very warm—no kind of day to be smelling smoke. When we got close enough to the fields to see where the smoke was coming from, we could see a helicopter sitting there. I was pretty concerned and annoyed about this.

At this point in my tale the family exploded with laughter and it was quite clear they felt I was being very restrained in describing my state of mind. Apparently they felt I should have admitted I was in a towering rage. At any rate, as Susan and I came into the fields we took a quick evaluating look at the fire burning in a stump along the edge of the clearing and decided we had time to go tie up the horses before getting buckets to put it out. In our hurry and panic we did something unprecedented. We led the horses in a straight line right across the hay field, cutting a swath through the foot-high hay crop. The two of us then raced to get water and put the fire out completely.

Then we saw someone in a blue shirt walking down towards the garden. Jack was down there, too, evidently having gone down to see what the man wanted. In the process of dousing the fire, I had knocked an oil can over and since I knew perfectly well it didn't belong to me, I was madder than ever by the time I saw the man with Jack and could scarcely wait to find out what was behind the strange goings-on. The dry birch stump in which the fire had clearly been intentionally set was only about 10 feet from dry balsam humus which in turn led up to the forest. There was a hint of wind and the temperature was around 80°F. As my mind took in all these facts the temperature in my immediate vicinity rose perceptibly!

Impulsively picking up a large stick from among those the fire had been fed with, I strode towards Jack and the stranger and demanded to know what was going on. The young man took one look and backed up the hill slightly. I guess he was perturbed at the appearance of one supremely angry small lady with a great stick clenched firmly in her hand!

He replied meekly that the helicopter had been headed for Tatla Lake from Vancouver. Spluttering on, he explained he had run out of gas because he had gotten off course. In reply to my insistence on knowing why on earth he had been stupid enough to light a fire, he blurted an incredible reply. "It's in the manual."

As he interpreted the instructions in the survival manual, the first thing to do when you come down in unfamiliar surroundings is to pour oil on a stump and set it ablaze! I yelped, "In *fire* season?" He replied quite reasonably, "I don't know anything about Canadian fire laws." Me—

"Where the devil do you come from?" Gulped the pilot, "L.A." Me—"What's *that*?"

The conversation from that point is unrecorded and according to contributing members of the family, it is also unrepeatable and decidedly unprintable!

It seemed the pilot did not have a compass or a radio and was incapable of reading a map. When Jack found him he was carrying a bridle and heading towards the garden. When the interloper caught sight of Jack he was obviously overjoyed to see a human being. He had at that time been lost for three days and had decided no one would be returning for a long time. He reached this conclusion despite the fact the dog was tied up in the barn. As a matter of fact, he had untied deaf old Skye and kept her by his side... either for company or moral support. He was admittedly terrified of wild beasts and yet had been quite prepared to take off on an unfamiliar horse with the avowed intention of heading south. This was the worst possible choice of direction as there is no human habitation for at least 80 miles, no trail and no way a horse could possibly get through.

He had missed all signs of the Edwards' spread just one and-a-half miles away and which he should have seen from the air on his approach. He ignored the fact that a bridge across a river might lead somewhere and the Highbanks bridge is quite visible from the upper storage room where he slept during his stay. He missed entirely the telephone wire that stretched away from the house and which would, presumably, lead somewhere.

After ascertaining all the clues he had disregarded and all the stupid conclusions he had leaped to, Jack decided the kindest thing he could do for the poor bemused man was put him on the trail for the Edwards' place so he could use the radio phone. His absence might have given me time to cool down but just at this point Susan emerged from where she had been preparing to put the horses away and reported another fire had been set in a second stump. This one was only 20 feet from the hay filled barn.

I got mad all over again—not that I'd really got over the first mad. (Susan threw in the comment that I had been so inflamed with fury it was surprising I didn't burn the barn down through spontaneous combustion!) Well, it would be bad enough to lose the barn but we certainly couldn't risk the lives of the horses as well. I circled the barn and examined every single stump anywhere near the building. Then I went into the hay loft and searched that carefully, too. I was plenty nervous.

After we put the horses away, Susan and I went back and made absolutely certain the other fire was totally extinguished. As we passed the helicopter which had both its doors open, I noticed some literature had blown out. I felt sort of guilty but couldn't resist looking at a *Memo to Pilots* from the Department of Transport. This pointed out that some complaints had been received from property owners in regard to helicopters landing on their land and creating a disturbance. It went on to recommend that pilots should take care not to annoy people in the event they had to put their craft down in any kind of emergency!

Two or three hours after he had left for the Edwards' farm, the pilot turned up back at our place, footsore in his cowboy boots and weary from the unaccustomed exercise. A great deal of time and patience was then expended by all concerned in an argument as to whether there was or was not a bridge across the river to The Birches. The pilot contended there was no such aid to permit him to traverse the river while we, who felt we knew just a little more about the situation than he, tried to convince him there was, indeed, just such a contrivance! The man could see the Edwards' place from the other side of the stream but had been unable to cross to it. He ended up going a full mile-and-a-half beyond where he needed to, before retracing his steps.

At this point a phone call was made on the intercom and Mrs. Edwards agreed to pass the message along that the pilot was downed and needed gas. This method of communication could have been used in the first place, of course, but it had seemed a good idea to get him out of the way for awhile.

While waiting for the rescue helicopter, the pilot was asked to move his craft to a spot where less damage would be done to the hay crop and small fruit trees by the rescue chopper which would set down beside the downed one. "He did what he was told, too", Susan chuckled. She took the short ride with him. The pilot spent the remainder of the afternoon sitting under the craft, presumably thinking over his sins of omission and commission. We put the man up for the night and fed him. The following morning, to keep him out of mischief, we enlisted his help in land-clearing, getting him to pick up branches. Susan complained he wasn't much help.

The other chopper arrived in the afternoon and its pilot expressed total incredulity at the fact the lost pilot had been there four days before getting a message out. Apparently he hadn't even filed his flight plan correctly so no one knew he had gone astray. This reminded Jack that during supper the previous night the pilot had expressed interest in listening to the news. He expected to hear the report of his being missing but no such item was aired.

In due time the refueling was completed and the rescue pilot took off. It took the other awhile to get his motor warmed up and his craft into position but eventually he followed. Since no report was ever broadcast about a missing chopper it is assumed he managed to follow-the-leader out of the valley and arrive safely!

When I concluded my story, someone wondered aloud how the pilot might relate the same tale.

"Probably describes this madwoman charging out of the woods at him like a wild beast, brandishing a club and yelling," volunteered Susan.

"Well, I was making some noises in the background he could probably hear. He probably deduced I wasn't happy," I admitted.

Susan commented that all the pilot had eaten was some cooked rhubarb, chocolate cake and stale bread he found in the verandah locker and this made her wonder aloud if he had gone thirsty or if he had noticed the river.

"He noticed he couldn't get across it at the Edwards' place," Jack observed mildly. He went on a trifle wistfully, "You know, when I first caught up with him carrying the bridle, he asked me if it was all right if he took the horse. I countered by asking if I could have the helicopter. He mumbled something about it being out of gas and it almost seemed that if there wasn't that small problem, I'd have been welcome to it."

Anyway, when all the laughter had died down, I had to admit I had been madder then than at any time in my life, and the scaredest, too. I couldn't stop thinking about the fact that the fire had been kept going for three days and that he was obviously prepared to just take off on a horse and leave it burning.

We discovered later that John Edwards had flown over, saw the fire, but assumed we knew what we were doing since he did not know we were away. He was surprised to learn that flares had been fired at him as he passed overhead.

15

Floods and other Disasters

If we aren't having problems with fires, there's always weather. The year 1965 provided enough trouble with the elements to last a lifetime.

Our packing routine at that time involved living at the north end of Stillwater while packing from Atnarko. We stockpiled freight until we had enough for a raft load. Then, while the horses rested for a day, we took the freight to the shed at the south end of Stillwater. One day we loaded the raft Spedar and put some stuff in the boat as well, then prepared to go up the lake. We customarily tie the boat alongside the raft as its motor is mounted on the stern. This time there was a slight breeze so we wanted to turn the raft around and get under way before tying the boat on. With Jack at the raft's motor and me at the bow with a long pole to push it around with, we started up. He was to hold the boat chain in one hand while operating the Evinrude with the other but somehow the end of the chain became entangled in the propellor. At that instant the south wind began to rise with startling rapidity. The motor stopped and as the water was 12 feet deep, poling was ineffectual. The raft and boat turned around and started downstream for the start of the rapids, 200 feet away. If the outfit had reached that point everything, us included, would have been smashed to bits.

Fortunately, there is a slight curve in the shoreline just

downstream of where our power failed and the wind, fast becoming a gale, drove us towards this point. Jack quickly clambered into the boat, paddling it close enough to shore to enable him to jump into the waist-deep water, grab a stump as an anchor and pull the raft closer to shore. As soon as Spedar swung close enough, I tied it to a stump. This left the raft stern-on to the rolling waves. Water was splashing over the partly filled boat, the motor on the raft and the back edge of the freight deck. Since the stuff was covered, we didn't think it would get wet. The boat's chain was snarled in the raft's outboard prop so we quickly unloaded onto the steep shore, then got it untangled. Susan was on the front of the raft and we had just taken her off when a dead tree broke off in the howling squall and crashed down right where she had stood minutes before.

As the exposed shore was not a good place to leave the raft we moved it, still loaded, a short distance downstream to where it was more sheltered. After packing the 600 pounds of boat freight about 100 feet back to the pile, we returned to the cabin to dry off and get warm.

During the night it rained, changing to snow just before dawn. This posed a new problem as the raft was so heavily laden the added weight of wet snow would sink it down and might get some of the freight wet. We went over with a broom at dawn and swept it clear.

Later in the day the snow stopped, the sun shone and we took the freight up to the other end of the lake without mishap. As this was only October 17 and the trees still had their yellow leaves, they made a strange but pretty sight bowed down under the clinging snow.

The weatherman had not played his final card. By October 20 we had finished packing to Stillwater from Atnarko and had moved to the south end of the lake with all the freight and the four horses. That afternoon we made a trip to Lonesome Lake with 1,000 pounds. By evening it was pouring rain so hard there was a constant roar over our heads. The roof leaked in a few places, too, so we hung pails under the streams to keep the water off our beds. The constant deluge kept up all night and in the morning the river was yellow-brown and rising fast.

We discovered later that Goat Creek which comes in at the north end of Stillwater had risen tremendously and brought down huge logs and rocks from its canyon. This completely blocked the Atnarko where it leaves Stillwater.

Jack made a trip to Lonesome Lake with another 1,000 pounds in the morning, despite the rain. Eventually it eased and finally stopped. All the small rivulets off the mountains were up and roaring. The big creek at the foot of Lonesome Lake was coming up fast, too, even though it had the long Turner Lake basin to act as a stabilizer and slow the rise. In the afternoon we all went up with another 1,000 pounds, and the creek at Lonesome Lake was so high it was beginning to roll boulders. Fortunately, it was broken up into several channels. If it had all been in one, we could never have crossed.

When we got back to Stillwater, we found the water already up three feet and rising three inches an hour. We knew we would have to get the entire 14,000 pounds out of the shed by 2 a.m. or it would get inundated. We gave the river until 10 that night but as it was still climbing then, we began to move the freight. We carried it, a 100-pound sack a trip each, about 100 feet to a tent on higher ground. A lantern in the shed and a lamp in the tent provided light. We moved 1,000 pounds into the tent and put the rest in the cabin. As we removed the last of it, the water was starting to advance across the sloping floor of the shed.

We cooked a meal then, as we were absolutely ravenous. Having worked half the night, we fell into bed. Tired as I was, I slept little for worrying about the freight we still had to get to Lonesome Lake. Susan slept through everything and at six in the morning we got up, prepared and ate breakfast and were ready to work as daylight crawled out from under its soggy blanket of fog.

Water covered all the horsefeed and the horses had retreated to the freight shed in order to get out of the deluge. We had to tie them up for the night or they would have gotten into the freight, not only ruining it, but probably making themselves sick from too much grain. It was the beginning of a fast for them, for we had oats enough to last only two days. They had cottonwood leaves with their oats for three additional days before we could get hay for them.

The river above the freight shed is ordinarily too fast to run a raft up but as the water rose, it became sluggish enough for us to take the loaded raft about a mile up the river to where we could use the trail. First thing in the morning we took the horses to higher ground, then made two raft trips with freight. Two or three boat trips sufficed to get all the stuff up to the new place, appropriately called Flood Point. By then it was nearly dark so we left the last load of freight on the raft for the night. Luckily it did not rain as we had not enough cover to properly shield all the piles strewn around the shore.

Just as we were starting to make camp I noticed the water had not risen for the past 15 minutes but dared not say anything for fear it would begin to rise again. Half-an-hour later it started falling and we could talk about it. Once the water began to drop, it fell at the same rate it had risen. All night long it ebbed steadily, making it necessary for us to get up every hour to re-tie the boat and raft so they wouldn't get left aground or break their ropes, causing everything to slide into the river.

By morning the river was steady. It had risen a total of eight feet before the Goat Creek dam cut-out and the water started down. It dropped a little more but remained about a foot-and-a-half above the pre-flood level. This left the trail to Lonesome Lake above water so we began packing again and all went well until we reached Lake Creek. Because of the lakes in its headwaters, this creek was slower in rising and even four days after the rain had stopped, it was still coming up. Lake Creek was making a noise like thunder and rolling boulders, any of which could have broken a horse's legs, even supposing we were able to force them into the raging torrent. Although we normally enjoy this creek, this was one time I wished it a thousand miles away.

We had to unpack the horses on the north side of the channels, cover the freight and after permitting the horses time to eat cottonwood leaves, return to Flood Point. We left the animals at the freight pile and went downriver to the cabin to stay overnight. We followed this routine for several days while waiting for the creek to assume more normal proportions.

After three days of restricted diet, the hapless horses were extremely hungry and would whinny pathetically at us as we moved around the camp. There were still oats but these had to be rationed until we could get more feed from home, which could not be done until the creek went down. All they had for breakfast was a little oats. They then packed their loads to the creek, ate leaves for two hours and returned to camp where they stood tied to trees with nothing further to eat all night.

Six days after the rain, Jack power-sawed a fir across the worst channel and since the others were down somewhat, we managed to get ourselves across Lake Creek and proceed to Lonesome Lake, where we found the 3,000 pounds of freight and our raft safe enough. The next day we rafted the horses across the river at Flood Point and turned them loose so they could find something to eat.

We headed for home, taking the 3,000 pounds of swan feed up the lake on the raft to the grain shed. We obtained some hay and oats from my parents and went back the next day, hunted up the horses and took them back across the river so we could begin packing again in the morning, leaving the hay at the foot of Lonesome Lake. We unpacked Thuja and I tried to ride her across the creek but hearing the rocks rolling and pounding, she refused to enter the foaming, swirling water. We looked around and found a place we could fix up as a horse crossing. Jack waded across, holding on to a rope I anchored on the bank. He cut a couple of poles and put them across the channel to form a bridge. At this place the water was not too fast for horses nor too deep for packs. We moved a lot of rocks in the icy water in an attempt to divert some of the flood into other channels. When all the horses were repacked we led them into the crossing, all their lead lines tied to a single rope. Jack crossed the bridge and I heaved the long rope across, enabling him to haul the reluctant horses over. They went better the next time but did not like the big rocks on the creek bed one bit, as they could not see them for foam and spray. The two geldings wallowed across and kept ducking their heads into the water until their halters became soggy and wet as old dish rags.

Having made an adequate crossing we went at the packing as fast as possible since late fall was pushing us. The weather behaved itself, the lake did not freeze early and our Mercury outboard did not fail us. We finally got everything home safe and dry.

With the fall packing and a few odd jobs done, the next job on our schedule is to put the horses out on range. This is a place south of Elbow Lake 10 to 15 miles south of here. We try to get the horses back home around Christmas time as the snow can get so deep they are unable to paw up a living.

153

More important, there is a rough piece of rockslide trail at the head of the lake which receives the full sweep of winter winds and the snow it picks up from the frozen lake gets piled in four- to six-foot drifts all along the trail, making it extremely difficult to get horses through.

Jack went up the first of January one year to get the horses and by the time he had located them two days later, this drift condition existed. He almost had to tunnel a trail through it for the horses. The groove he made with his chest and knees was just wide enough for them and their ears were all that could be seen above the snow. They were very calm and just followed along in the ditch with the snow pressing in against their sides. He led the first horse and the two others followed. The entire 500-foot distance took two full hours to cross. Once past this, the trail goes through timber so there was no more drifting and only about 18 inches of snow to plough through. He couldn't use snowshoes for the job as horses being led tend to step on the tails of the shoes and either break them or throw the person on his face in the snow—neither of which is desirable. Jack got home that night more tired than I had ever seen anyone. Needless to say, we now try to get them in a little earlier.

When we brought the horses in from the range in the fall of 1967, Rommy was so thin we left him at Fogswamp to eat hay in the dry barn and put the other three on my mother's slough grass fields and the islands at the head of Lonesome Lake. Each day when Rommy was let out of the barn he would stand at the fence and look longingly down the trail for the other horses. We eventually decided he would be better off happy and wet than dry and lonely. Jack took him down to join the other horses who obviously were as glad to see Rommy as he was to see them. He seemed to do all right then except for the fact that his teeth were so worn down he couldn't feed properly. It took him so long to eat the amount he needed, there just weren't enough hours in the day, so he was slowly starving.

Just past the middle of January the weather began to be wet and on one particularly nasty day, Jack decided to bring all the horses home. When he returned from feeding the swans that day, all the horses were in the field bordering Big Lagoon, so he caught Thuja and started off. Rommy would not follow but just stuck his head in a willow bush and stood there. Jack turned back for him, leading Thuja by her mane, as he had only one rope. When he got off the field and onto the trail on the hillside, he drove Thuja ahead of him and led Rommy, and the other two horses followed behind. They had only a mile-and-a-half to travel but old Rommy had to stop and rest so often the trip back home took about two hours. Jack left Rommy on the trail about half-a-mile from the barn while he brought the others up. They didn't want to leave the old horse, apparently believing he needed them for protection in his weakened condition but Jack figured Rommy would come up by himself in time. Jack was soaked to the skin from the drenching downpour and getting colder each time he had to wait for Rommy, who kept taking about 10 minutes' rest before he could be persuaded to walk slowly a further 100 feet. We gave him three hours to come home. He hadn't made it by then and as we didn't want him to spend the night in the filthy weather I took a light hand-gun and went down to see what was the matter with him. I found him trying to eat some snow-downed birch twigs only about 400 feet closer to home than Jack had left him. He was soaking wet, skinny as a rail fence and hungry, yet when I came up to him and he saw me, he whinnied cheerfully. The sound drove a knife into my heart. I gave him a carrot and he chomped it up. I then put a halter on him and started off to see if he could make it home and perhaps get a few more weeks of life. Clearly it wouldn't be more than that. He would go only about 30 feet without resting and it soon became painfully clear what I had to do.

I led my old friend off the road, tied him to a tree and ended his life with a single bullet, hoping like the devil it was the best thing for him, although I felt like a murderer and a traitor. I am certain he knew nothing of my intentions and never knew what hit him. I wanted to be with him during his last minute alive. He was born when I was 14 years old and his life spanned two-thirds of my own. I learned to ride on his round back and it was I who trained him. He was a true friend and had survived a long time for a horse—almost a quarter of a century.

Two days later we took the three remaining horses back to the head of the lake and shoved them into the river so they would cross to some islands where there was good grass. They were only half-way across the river when it began to rain again, as it continued to do all the rest of the day and night.

155

The following morning it was still pouring. Bear Bath Creek which runs through our place was up, running all over the fields. When we opened the front door a couple of hours before daylight, we saw water running down the trail right to the door. The muddy stream was lapping at the floor planks and was over some at the end of the house. We went out the back door and water was there, too. Evil-looking black liquid was all around the house and under it as well. The rich soil that colored it was our own land from a new clearing we had seeded the previous spring for pasture. Together with the cows, we had created a trail through the snow from the barn to the creek, past the house. This trail was made of hard-packed snow and formed a dike running all the way across the field. The water spread over the field, hit the dike, backed up and finally ran over into the trail which it followed right in through the front gate and on to the front door.

Jack donned a pair of 30-inch boots, waded out and cut a ditch through the snow dike so the water could run straight across to the river. After breakfast Jack started down to feed the swans but when he got part way down the road he realized how much the river had risen. He became concerned the horses might not get off the low land we had put them on, as to do so they would have to jump into the icewater that was looking more and more like liquid soil. He returned and collected Susan and me. Susan could not do much to help, of course, but we couldn't leave her in the house all day by herself, either. It was raining and cold, about 36°F.

Down we all went, Jack carrying Susan on his back where the water was over the road and me breaking trail through the water-soaked 16-inch-deep snow slush. Small creeks had backed up and the water was being held on the flat ground by the deep solid snow. Jack's hip-waders filled as soon as he got into the deep water.

It was extremely cold and before long our feet and legs were numb. Skye had come along with us as I had not realized the condition of the road or how much trouble she would have wallowing in the soggy stuff. Still, she gamely made it all the way down and home again.

When we got to Big Lagoon, the water had risen so much the ice had broken loose from the shore all the way around and the only place we could get on was where a log lay out from the shore. Jack had to go across to the Edwards' airplane hangar to rescue some mail we had left there in hopes of it catching a flight out. Susan and I went on down the ice. There was so much water at the grain shed we had to launch the boat to get across the channel to feed the swans in shallower water.

Next, we went looking for the horses. Lucky heard us while we were feeding the swans but we could scarcely hear his whinny above the noise of the roaring waterfalls on the mountain. We had gone only a short distance when I spotted the horses huddled together in fetlock deep water, on the driest part of their island. Jack rowed the boat right up to them, got out and caught Thuja and Rocket. For once, Rocket was glad to be caught! They were shivering like aspens in a breeze from all the water on top of them combined with having their feet in ice-water. Even tough little Rocket was shaking. I mounted Thuja from the stern of the boat and forced the horses to slog through the black water to the other end of the island. From there we could cross them to the grain shed and a trail home. Jack and Susan brought the boat around to the crossing place. I jumped off Thuja and into the boat. First we tried to swim both mares at once but the river was so fast that while we were trying to get them off the vertical bank, the boat drifted so far downstream their ropes got tangled with a small bush on the bank. Thuja was already in the river but we couldn't entice Rocket in so I slipped the rope off Thuja and let her go so she wouldn't drown. She jumped right back on the bank and sloshed off to investigate some grass sticking out of the water. I cut the bush free, Jack rowed the boat farther upstream and we pulled Rocket off into the river. As soon as Lucky heard her go in, he came running and plunged into the water almost on top of Rocket's rump. Thuja, who was farther away, came running too and jumped off the bank with a muddy splash. Left to themselves, not a single one of them would have entered the river. As soon as one went in, however, the others were eager to follow. They swam across the 100-foot channel, trying to leap out of the frigid water even as they swam.

They could scarcely walk for shivering, so as soon as we got them to the grain shed we got dry sacks and rubbed their chests and necks as hard as possible. I walked Rocket and Thuja around as fast as I could make them go, Lucky trailing after. Meanwhile, Jack got a fire going for Susan, me, and the horses. While they warmed up, Jack sanded the icy sections of the trail so the horses would not slide off and get hurt.

Meanwhile, the rain continued.

As it was impossible to get the horses onto Big Lagoon ice, it was necessary to take them around on the low-water trail. In places Jack found the water six inches above his hip waders. I was soaked again getting the horses off the bank of the river. We were both cold and miserable. The rain didn't slacken all day and the black water-laden clouds hung heavy and brooding along the valley. When we got to where the water covered the road, I rode Thuja and took Susan behind me so Jack wouldn't have to carry her over the slippery slush trail. We arrived home at five o'clock, cold and wet, but with the horses safe. And the rain kept falling.

About six the next morning we looked out of our kitchen window and saw not little Bear Bath Creek, but the whole Atnarko River coming across the field!

It had climbed two feet overnight and was still coming up as the ceaseless downpour continued. This new channel was going past the bank 10 feet from the east side of the house at a speed of four miles an hour, only 10 inches below the level of the house. The whole river had risen so high it dammed one of its channels south of our place and was forced into an old dry one which came straight down over the fields and past the house. All the field area between the house and the river was under muddy water by the time it stopped coming up. It melted the snow wherever it ran, leaving knolls and wreaths of snow to mark its passage.

As the rain fell and the water rose, we seriously considered the need to move to higher ground. We began moving stuff upstairs and collecting whatever we felt would be needed if we had to evacuate. The water kept on rising at a rate of about two inches an hour and was filled with forest debris together with many of the logs and stumps we had so laboriously placed along the river bank to try and restrain it.

About ten o'clock the rain ended. Still the river kept inching upwards, the rate of climb not even slowing for some time. By three in the afternoon we noticed the water was no longer climbing our picket fence. It slowly started down. As it did so, all the rubble from over the fields piled three or four feet deep against the fence back of the woodshed.

At its crest the river was about 400 feet wide and ranged in depth from three feet over the flooded fields to eight feet in its own channels. This was the worst flood in at least 50 years. Altogether it rose two feet higher than the summer maximum and there was only a foot leeway before it would have covered our floor.

On our trips up and down the valley that spring we saw where many ordinarily small streams had risen tremendously, snapping off cedar and cottonwood up to a foot in diameter. Other creeks had piled up boulder bars.

The flood in 1968 comprised much more water than either the '36 or the '65 floods as those had been partially caused by some of the lakes being dammed, whereas this one was all water! There was so much of it in the Atnarko it not only took out the Goat Creek dam but went on to dredge the one formed by the flood three years previously and actually lowered Stillwater in the process.

During the inundation many mice were run out of their burrows in the fields and came to our house to survive. While trying to save itself from drowning one ran out on the saturated snow and darted over the surface. A whisky jack saw it, killed it and ate it. I didn't know whisky jacks were birds of prey, but that one certainly was.

As soon as it stopped raining an Arctic storm blew in. Two days later the temperature was down to only 4°F. The sudden drop caused all land still under water to get covered with ice. I feared for the tame grass in the bare fields but it was tougher than I thought. There was very little die-off.

One year there was a disaster which changed the configuration of a huge section of the valley although it did not involve either fire or flood.

The Atnarko River which runs through ours and the Edwards' properties originates about 16 miles south of Lonesome Lake in a small glacial lake, 3,000 feet above the valley floor. The creek from this lake roars down the timbered slope, disappears into the trees and almost vanishes until it reaches the valley bottom, its initial mad rush by then considerably slowed. It continues at a sedate pace between banks of glacial mud formed by a much larger creek which comes in from the west.

The western stream is a wild one, going nearly dry during cold winter months but becoming a raging white torrent in July or during a prolonged rain. It has a large valley with a glacier at the head of it at an elevation of around 8,000 feet.

This creek was unpredictable. Some years it would flow into Knot Lake while others it would flow north and enlarge the Atnarko River. Where the two creeks join, the valley floor is about half-a-mile wide and used to be densely forested with large cottonwood, spruce, cedar and Douglas fir.

In the summer of 1959 a huge slide out of Westcreek brought down millions of tons of rock and trees, bulldozing right across the valley floor. After pushing over the stand of 80- to 110-foot-high trees, it still had enough momentum to climb the 20 degree slope on the opposite side for a distance of several hundred feet. Some of the shattered chunks of cliff brought down at that time are blocks larger than 20 x 30 feet. Several such immense pieces of granite were carried almost the full half-mile across the valley bottom after tearing out of the Westcreek's own valley which enters at a right angle. All signs of vegetation were torn from West-creek valley and up both sides for a good distance. As the valley is sinuous, the slide rose higher when it piled up on itself, making the turns, scraping the walls clean in places to a height of 400 feet above the new creek level. A huge amount of slide debris poured into the head of Knot Lake and caused a tidal wave which smashed off trees for a height of eight to 10 feet all around the lakeshore. The slide created a dam preventing the creek from the east from flowing into Knot Lake and making its natural course north into the Atnarko. Westcreek, on the other hand, can go either way, depending on how it happens to pile its rocks and logs. If it comes north, the Atnarko runs white but if it goes into Knot Lake, Atnarko remains clear except at high water, when it turns brown.

The Federal Fisheries Department was interested in making Westcreek run into Knot Lake, as Atnarko is an important salmon spawning stream and they believe glacial silt to be harmful to salmon eggs. Jack worked with the Fisheries Department on their first attempt to control the creek. They carried a total of two tons of rock in their arms from as far away as 90 feet. All this rock was piled up to form a 40-foot dike of boulders, some of which weigh 140 pounds. The dam was intended to divert the creek into Knot Lake, but the very first high water removed it. Several years later the Fisheries Department went in with large equipment and helicopters to build another dam. This one presumably is more effective as it has survived two floods.

T24L-50.

Looking south down the Atnarko River we are surrounded by the Coast Mountain Range of central British Columbia. Chilcotin Plateau extends eastward to left while Coast Range deeply indented by long fiords extends westward to Pacific Ocean. The first lake is Stillwater. Lonesome Lake snakes along below Turner Lake nearly 2000 feet above. Hunlen Falls empty out of the north end. *The Birches,* the Edwards' homestead, is at the south end of Lonesome Lake while *Fogswamp* is one and a half miles farther south upstream on the Atnarko.

Coast Mountain snow
fields feed the Atnarko
River and many other
raging rivers flowing into
Pacific Ocean. Peak runoff
and high water on rivers is
May and June.

Atnarko River passing through *Fogswamp*.

Hunlen Falls dropping more than 1300 feet from Turner Lake to the Atnarko River.

Typical coastal fiord that penetrates 50 or more miles inland to the snow clad Coastal Mountains.

Left to right—Ruth McVeigh, Susan Hancock, Trudy Turner, Jack Turner and daughter Susan saying goodbye as Ruth, Susan and publishers David and Susan Hancock prepare to walk 30 miles out to highway.

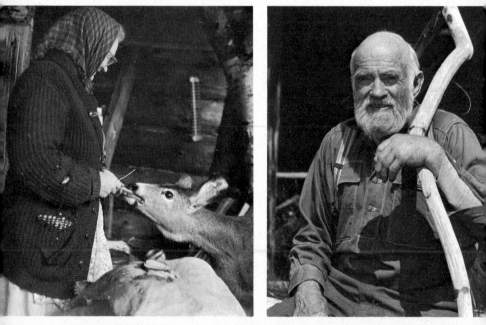

Ethel and Ralph Edwards also lived a life of close association with wild animals and hard work--essential values for surviving in the wilderness.

Trudy as a teenager displaying fine harvest of corn. Note profusion of flowers outside home.

Trudy proudly stands on float of the plane she had gone 'outside' to buy so she and her father would no longer be confined to walking.

Ralph re-fueling in Bella Coola.

Grizzly bear abound on the Atnarko River--here seen walking across the *Fogswamp* homestead to fish the river.

Buck deer in velvet investigates Trudy as she builds her first home at *Fogswamp.*

Black bear are also common in area.

Beaver--the only other forester inhabiting *Fogswamp.*

Clark's nutcracker forages for scraps along with gray jays around house and barn.

Ruffed or willow grouse struts and drums for his ladyfriends and the Turners.

Deer are so tame they become a nuisance in eating garden or hard-earned pasture grass.

Trudy and Skye beside her newly finished cabin--her first home at *Fogswamp*.

Looking northwest to house and barn under construction. Note piles of roots protecting bank of Atnarko River from erosion during flood.

Fogswamp

The barn.

Wood shed under construction. Hand split shakes were carried in by Thuja and Rommy.

Trudy inspecting new calf.

Winter's quiet beauty with its long dark nights: a time to practice music lessons, read, and play records.

Trudy, Jack and Susan share all chores outdoors and inside. Trudy specializes in carving wood--either animals or furniture.

Winter is also a time for Trudy to paint. Her works reflect her love of horses and wildlife.

Concern for living things is carried to extremes most people aren't prepared to take: the two family male cats (so as not to encourage feral ones) are tied up each day during the bird migration season so they confine their activities to catching mice at night. Each cat has his own insulated box.

The total effort of building houses, barns, numerous out buildings plus miles of fencing doesn't prevent the Turners from attending to detail such as this deer antler gate hinge.

Fogswamp baby buggies: Susan at one month arrives home.

...at 15 months

...at 2½ years.

Growing up at *Fogswamp*.

Susan at 17 years still shares a very strong bond with the animals...and with Trudy and Jack it is the bond of life.

Everything comes and goes from *Fogswamp* on the back of either horse or human.

Mower wheels.

Jack carrying 10-foot plywood sheets for boat. When carrying 14-foot sections earlier he encountered grizzly bear on trail.

Leading cow to safety during flood.

Launching boat to travel down Lonesome Lake.

Pack train hauling in 4 years supply of bought food.

Traveling down the Stillwater.

Pack train barged down Lonesome Lake.

Harvesting crops can't begin until the great forests are cut and cleared away. The first hay crops are planted between stumps.

Disking.

Mowing

Raking--wheels were backpacked 35 miles into *Fogswamp* by Jack.

The bountiful garden provides not only the year's potatoes and vegetables but a generous show of beautiful flowers.

Hauling in the hay.

For holidays the Turners just climb up to Turner Lake above for camping and horseback riding above timberline.

Miscellaneous winter bounty--a fascinating ice ring forms each year on a backeddy on the Atnarko just below Fogswamp. The slowly circling ice increases in size until it hits shore.

The Atnarko is home for all five species of salmon and three species of trout-- a great food source to the bears *and* Turners.

Lonesome Lake got world attention when Ralph Ewards started to offer winter feed to these magnificent and very rare birds. This project later got support from conservation societies and provincial and federal wildlife authorities. Trudy took over the project as a small girl and swan-feeding and winter are synonymous. The birds breed in the Rocky Mountains and arrive at Lonesome Lake in late winter, remaining until breakup in March.

Whistling swan.

Mute swan.

TOM W. HA

Trumpeters wait at feeding station.

Trudy feeding: each swan gets half-pound of grain daily. By late season and in colder weather, swans become very tame--stealing grain when Trudy's back is turned.

Swans either scoop grain up off ice with side of their great bills or reach underwater to retrieve it from the muddy bottom.

Adult swans are white--immatures gray-brown.

With the onset of spring the birds are more belligerent and fights frequently break out.

Susan is obviously also a trusted member of the unusual Lonesome Lake family.

Young cygnet comes for a handout but 30° below weather is so cold he stops to tuck feet up under body to warm them.

Whether caring for an abandoned saw-whet owl or taking a rare pose with Susan in front of her swans, Trudy Turner represents trust and dependability that are a way of life.

Knot Lake is the division of the watersheds of the Bella Coola and the Klinaklini Rivers. The river flowing out of this lake races south between ever higher and snowier mountains until it merges with the Klinaklini in a wide, flat valley. The enlarged river meanders about 23 miles through willow-lined mudbanks. In the spring the trumpeter swans feed in the shallow lakes dotting the valley floor. The valley narrows to a canyon with vertical granite walls while the river it contains hurtles along over low falls, log jams and around sharp turns of rock for about 10 miles. It then unites with the mighty Klinaklini glacier, a river of ridged, blue-green ice, streaked with glacial debris. The silty water flows along braided stream channels to the head of Knight inlet, 14 miles distant.

I have piloted a plane over this region several times and always enjoyed the awe-inspiring spectacle of snow, ice and perpendicular granite, glacier and waterfall. Seen from 6 or 7,000 feet, just as the sun is setting, the two snow-covered peaks of Mt. Waddington (13,177 feet) and Monarch Mountain (11,599 feet) appear as tall golden spires against a background of blue.

The extremely rugged wild beauty, a sea of sharp glistening peaks as far as the eye could see, was unforgettable. Directly under the fragile T-craft's belly ran the green valley and the slowly winding river. There is actually a valley through from the head of Knight Inlet to the head of North Bentinck Arm. The highest point in the valley is on the Westcreek slide at an elevation of about 1,800 feet. Heading north on the Atnarko River, the 30- or 40-foot wide stream snakes its way toward the next lake. A few miles from Knot Lake the Atnarko is joined by a white stream from the west, then continues to Elbow Lake where the mountains are relatively low. After a quarter-mile of rapids Rainbow Lake can be seen, a three-mile-long body of water with white sand beaches on the west side. Goat bluffs lie along the east side and rise to form the 8,000 foot Mt. Ada. The western slopes are deeply cut by streams which form the beaches. Trumpeter swans spend some time feeding in the inlets and outlet of this lake. From here the river roars and rushes until it enters Tenas Lake, another place where the swans find shallow feeding grounds.

16

Vigorous Vacations

Climbing the mountains surrounding Fogswamp is our favorite form of recreation, one we seldom have time to enjoy more than a few days each year. We climb mountains, not just because they are there, but because we are over-whelmingly curious to know exactly *what* is there!

Every trip is different and every single step of the way differs from every other. The entire area surrounding us is pocked with tiny lakes and valleys with patches of flowers, interesting rock formations and dangerous challenges. There are birds and animals to observe, new faces of familiar mountains to view and the close interdependence of our family to enjoy.

In 1965 we climbed to the top of 7,000-foot Trumpeter Mountain east of us. We started out before sunrise and by lunchtime were above timberline where a few snowbanks still oozed water. Once out of the valley the scene becomes one of rolling alpine country with many wet flower-strewn meadows. This is easy walking and one can see about 40 miles in all directions. The ground is covered with heather, moss, short yellowish grass and about 17 different kinds of flowers including lupines, marsh marigolds and buttercups. Bird life is lavish, too. Robins, rosy finch, white and yellow-crowned sparrows and horned larks spring up almost at one's feet and dart away.

We made camp on a long moraine and watched the sunset

fill the tranquil western sky while the birds sang and the mosquitoes buzzed. As it was the end of June there was only a little frost on the meadows in the morning when we awoke to the murmuring of two small streams bracketing our camp. The one on the south side tasted like dissolved lichens while the other was sweet. We climbed into the sunshine for breakfast and sat on grass-covered benches while the faithful mosquitoes followed, looking for their morning meal. As soon as we reached the top of the ridge, all the bugs left us.

There are only a few dwarf trees above the tree line because of harsh conditions and the short growing season. If they grew taller the part sticking out of the snow would get cut back by the blasts of winter wind that sweep across the unprotected mountain top. Judging by tracks gouged deeply into the soft surface of every wet place, many moose live in the high meadows, thriving on alpine birch and meadow grass.

We headed for home the second day, my flower pail filled with specimens I wished to paint.

All we ever carry for shelter on our trips is a piece of fairly heavy plastic, 10 feet square, equipped with grommets and strings. By securing one side along the rope and the other along a log on the ground, the plastic forms a lean-to which adequately covers the three of us, plus our packs.

We pored over air photos and the excellent map put out by the Department of Mines and Technical Surveys before we took off on our next trip, a three-day excursion which would take us to Turner Lake, from where we would proceed to a small lake at the head of Goat Creek.

Turner Lake, the name of which has no connection with us, is the largest body of water on the flat land which occurs at the 3,500-foot elevation. It is nearly four miles long. My father stocked it with cutthroat in 1949. Now there are many nice trout in the entire string of seven lakes, spread over a length of about 11 miles. The water from Turner Lake boils down a steep river for about 200 feet, then disappears over a wall to free-fall almost 1,000 feet as a solid sheet of water about 20 feet wide until it turns to spray, some of which drifts back all the way to the top of the canyon walls, watering the moss and trees growing on every ledge, nook and cranny within its range. When the water is high it creates a stront wind and some of the spray is blown right out of the canyon. The surrounding lush growth of grass, brush and other vegetation makes good pasturage for mountain goats which live on the canyon walls wherever it is wide enough for them to walk. Obviously they don't require much room for they have trails up some of the steepest places where there is only the most meager ledge to cling to. A pinnacle of rock sticks up in the middle of the falls where it drops over the rim. It splits the water during dry seasons but during flood the whole falls is a smooth, fluid rush. Standing on a shoulder of the mountain a quarter-of-a-mile away the water can be heard as a constant thundering roar and one can almost feel the rocks tremble underfoot. During winter the spray turns to ice. A huge pile builds, sometimes reaching all the way to the top and forming great blue curtains. The ice can take until July to melt completely. The falls drop behind the ice, coming out from under the mass some distance downstream. Occasionally the ice builds in a cone shape with a peak where the water vanishes behind it. At intervals, long spouts of water come out the sides of the dome through fissures in the ice. There may be several of these coming out in various places, each running for only a few seconds then reappearing out of a different set of openings in the ice.

We started out on another trek early one bright August morning, heading out the road almost to the Venturi Bridge then cutting back through the forest to the base of the mountain and tracing a small creek to a graded trail. After reaching the flat cradling Turner Lake we continued along the winding trail over dry pine ridges through open meadows, ending abruptly on the bank of Hunlen Creek.

My brother John uses this trail to get to his tourist cabins which are located on a beautiful white sand beach on the west side of Turner Lake. He has a dock and several good boats with outboards for use on the lake. The boats eliminate his need for a trail beyond the creek we reached and since it was only knee deep and narrow, we waded across and pushed on until mid-morning by which time we were approaching John's resort where a small stream flowed through the pines. We ate lunch before going to ask John about the 6,000-foot elevation Carol Lake, a small body of water with glaciers to the south of it, where we intended to camp that night.

John interrupted his work long enough to give Susan a ride in one of the boats, then we continued on our way. After travelling for hours through dense lodgepole pines, balsam, spruce and white bark pine, we encountered a forest of old-growth pines, some of which were two feet in diameter. At this point the lush undergrowth of blueberries we had been enjoying for some time, petered out. Some of them were an inch-and-a-half around, and absolutely delicious.

On the sub-alpine level, blue lupines still bloomed among the pine and balsam trees. The higher we climbed the more varieties of flowers we observed until we reached the open uplands sloping at an even steeper angle to the broken crest of a 6,500-7,000-foot range west of Turner Lake.

Carol Lake lay around the north end of the peak ahead of us. Eroded hollows and rock piles marked that side of the mountain which led to a flower-edged stream tinkling downhill for about 100 yards to a smaller, almost circular greenish-blue lake which became known to us as Moss Lake. Upstream through yellow and purple flowers the creek, where it pours out of Carol Lake, is almost four feet wide with flower-decked mossy banks. The creek bed itself is composed of large black algae-covered stones.

Carol Lake is pear-shaped, half-a-mile long, with raw, glacier-strewn moraines coming right to the water's edge along part of the shoreline while huge chunks of ice lie out over the water under black outcrops on the other end. The lake is in a basin, the walls on the south and west side rising up to steep, scoured cliffs under which lie grooved, bluish glaciers. A flat-topped ridge sloping up from the shore is covered with short grass, lichens, heather and flowers. We had our second meal of the day at the outlet of Carol Lake. Susan used a flat stone for a plate to eat her portion of "alpine meat loaf", a concoction of fresh corn, peas, eggs, bear meat, potato, onion, salt and pepper all mixed up, pressed into a loaf pan and baked. It is very good and moist. We ate slices of it with our bread. Cookies washed down with clear glacial water were our dessert

Leaving our packs behind we angled up to the ridge to gaze down into Goat Creek valley, a basin of pastoral beauty and raw ruggedness. Naked moraines of worn boulders ran down from broken bluffs to flatten out and give way to grassy meadows. The streams winding across them fall over the edge of the steep valley of Goat Creek. After admiring and photographing the view, we moved on. The sun was getting low so our shadows were several times our length. As we turned eastward, they stretched out grotesquely before us.

There was not much daylight left after we reclaimed our packs so we had to hurry to set up our tent although the sky gave no indication of rain. At that altitude and lacking forest cover there would be a heavy dew if not actual frost, so we wanted a roof. The only piece of ground smooth and soft enough to sleep on was way out in the middle of the grassy slope, well away from trees. We had to improvise with piles of rocks to support and brace the poles. The shelter must have been set up securely enough, for it was tested pretty severely during the night. After several hours of trying to accommodate our bodies to the ditches and ridges on which we were attempting to sleep, Jack and I were awakened by some great force pushing the plastic down onto our faces. A strong wind was blasting down from the cliffs, whipping the surface of the small lake into whitecaps and doing its best to blow down our shelter. Eventually the morning dawned bright, clear and so calm Carol Lake seemed a mirror before us.

After breakfast we went along the ridge to where it rose up black, narrow and broken. Huge, sharply angled rocks, precariously piled, threatened to plummet down to the lake below, preventing any southerly progress on our part. We headed down to try to traverse the Turner Lake side of the mountain on a goat trail covered with grass and flowers. We were searching for a route back to the top but had not discovered one, so headed for Junker Lake further up Hunlen Creek. A long slide of sharp sand and small rock ran far down the mountain so we simply plunged down this, raising a choking yellow dust behind us. The dirt slide connected with a snowslide path which we followed as far as the timber, eventually reaching pine forest. Under the trees was foot-high grass so walking was easy until we came out of the park-like setting and into dense pines, spruces, swamps and Labrador Tea. We forded the creek below Junker Lake outlet and half-an-hour later were on the western end of the golden crescent beach. Being pretty tired, we just walked up the beach and set up camp, making our beds in the sand and then reclining on them to admire majestic Talchako Mountain.

About the only surface harder than beach sand is concrete, so we awoke quite often that night, trying to persuade the unyielding material to give way just a little under our hips and shoulders. Still, there were compensations. Each time we wakened, we admired the huge mountains and their mirrored images in the placid moonlit water. A loon called sweetly one time and early in the morning an ungainly heron flopped languidly along several feet above the beach, its long legs trailing behind like an afterthought! Several sandpipers ran busily along the edge of the water picking insects out of the trash some thoughtless earlier visitor had left on the wet sand.

We had noticed Skye was limping from wearing out her paws on the steep dirt slides the previous day so with pieces of one of our sacks, I made shoes for her so she could get home in relative comfort. They were just squares of material folded over her paws and tied round her legs but they stayed on fairly well until we ran into dense timber, swamps and windfall. We let her go "barepaw" until we reached the trail, then I put them back on until we arrived at our place.

From the time we get home after one such expedition until we leave for the next one, we derive enjoyment recalling what we have seen and making plans for the area we want to explore next time.

We crawled expectantly out of bed bright and early one August morning a year after the last trip, the sky promising a fine day for our third mountain trip in two years. A few fluffy cumulus clouds, slightly tinged with yellow, floated across the opalescent dawn. We prepared and ate breakfast, fixed the hens for a two-day absence, then started off just as the top of our goal, Walker's Dome, changed from golden rose to dull gold. We wanted to leave the horses, Thuja and Rocket, at the head of Tenas Lake, so we took them up there and put them on pasture, then started up the mountain. It was still cool and even though we had fairly heavy packs, climbing the thickly timbered slope was not difficult. After an hour or so the sun was on us and we were panting.

This time we were heading for a glacial basin on the east side of Walker's Dome just above timberline, roughly 5,000 feet. A small clear creek down in a narrow box canyon was our guide. We would follow it nearly all the way to the basin, sometimes 100 feet above it on the steeply sloping yellow sand bank and sometimes right on the creek bottom, clambering over algae and moss-covered stair-steps of water-worn granite. There were always ledges and cracks on the surface of the rocks to use for hand and toe holds. The creek was profusely bordered on both sides by alpine fireweed, known locally as "river beauty". Interspersed with this were monkey flowers, brilliant yellow slipper-like blooms more than an inch long, their throats adorned with brown spots and hairs. Clear water trickled and splashed over the smooth, mossy dark stones in the bottom of the creek bed, contrasting with the bright flowers. In these surroundings we ate our lunch while Skye lay in the shade of the bank. After cooling a few minutes she began poking in the water in search of something to play with.

We continued our climb after eating, the fir forest gradually giving way to lodgepole pine which in turn surrendered to short balsam trees and white bark pine. A little below timberline we were forced out of the creek bed by vertical canyon walls and had to detour through the forest. The last 500 or so feet were ascended rather slowly due to four-foot-high false rhododendron, a pale greenish-yellow flowered member of the heath family which formed a dense jungle beneath the pines. We could not even see the ground and had to plow ahead blindly, stepping on fallen logs, rocks and into unseen holes. Eventually we broke out of the undergrowth to see before us the nearly treeless rim of the hollow we were looking for a small distance across a solid green and white carpet of heather, dwarf alpine balsam and mountain ash. The cirque, raw and ice-ravaged, ran upward between steep granite cliffs and ice-scrubbed rockslides, coming to an abrupt halt at an immense boulder pile at the base of a 200-foot vertical rock wall. Using the remains of last winter's snow, we cooled off by throwing snowballs at one another and at Skye! Blooming right next the snow were mountain laurel, bluebells and purple asters.

Working over to the north side of the basin, we passed a small rock-bottomed blue lake surrounded by clean slabs. Each year the ice and snow move the rocks so much nothing can grow on them. We started climbing straight up the rocky slope. As many of the boulders were insecure, we had to test each one to be sure it would not roll and catch our feet or start a slide. Near the top about 1,000 feet above the basin floor, we had to negotiate a rock chimney. On each side, sheer rock walls rose up 20 feet while a stream of water oozed through loose rock and sand underfoot. After photographing the flowers, moss and green grass clinging tenaciously to tiny cracks in the broken white granite, we emerged at last on top of a smooth sloping ridge. From here we could look north along the Turner Lake area and Atnarko Valley although clouds kept us from seeing the mountains to the northeast very clearly. Mt. Ada, across the valley from us, stood out sharply.

From this point the slope dropped toward Lonesome Lake, levelling off on the Turner Lake flat. Behind us the ridge ran uphill to eventually disappear under a white sheet of ice and snow. Everywhere streams wandered about seeking a place to jump off the cliffs into cirques and basins from which they tumbled down through dark green timber to form pot-hole meadows before joining up with larger streams, eventually wending their way to the sea.

The elevation of the ridge was close to 6,500 feet. Few flowers grew there as the snow had long since melted off and the ground was quite dry. Clumps of moss-like plants with small purple flowers were about all we saw outside of the omnipresent black lichens. Far below us was a rock-rimmed cirque containing stunted balsams and grass as short as that on a putting green. A small lake appeared the typical bluish-green of mountain lakes even under the now-cloudy sky. The meadow stretched away down the hill towards Junker Lake.

At this point Susan informed us she was hungry so Jack took out half a square of chocolate for her. As soon as she took a bite, Susan made a hideous face and announced in incredulous tones that it was *bitter*! Apparently we had got the two kinds mixed, but as the bag also contained several squares of the semi-sweet variety, Susan had her snack.

We started up the gentle slope toward a long medial moraine passing many house-sized chunks of rock perched perilously on the brink, looking as though a light wind would send them rumbling to the bottom. They must fall off frequently during the spring as we hear some awesome noises from the old mountain at that time of year. Following a goat trail along a steep ridge, we reached the base of the moraine where snow hiding in the shadows was pink with algae and streaked with mud. The moraine, a great heap of rocks piled haphazardly one on top of another, stretched away toward a long, smooth snow-white glacier lying on a higher elevation. We found a place where we were able to crawl up between the truck-sized monoliths to gain the top of the dike.

By this time we were all quite hungry and since water would be scarce further up, we spread our lunch on a large rock and ate. The entire area was covered with mountain goat tracks. A few grizzlies had sunk their huge paws deep into the soft gray-brown mud as they waddled past the small lake.

We had planned to climb to the highest peak on the mountain (about 8,250 feet) but after starting up the slide and finding it very loosely composed, we changed our minds. We considered a number of alternative routes, but eventually decided to go up the rock slide after all, creeping along cautiously, testing each rock before putting our weight on it. The whole 45 degree slope looked as if it would start rolling down onto the glacier if we so much as coughed. By the time it became evident we should never have attempted the project, we were more than half-way up, so we pressed on. When we reached safer terrain, Jack took a picture looking back down the glacier.

We dumped our packs and walked until we could look down on Kidney Lake on Hunlen Creek and across to the rough peaks with their snow cowls, west of the Talchako River. A high mass of black granite reared up to the south. A large, heavily crevassed glacier filled the valley from wall to wall and extended up the flank of the opposite peak at least half-way to its rounded top. Directly below us was a divide where the glacier oozed eastwards toward Atnarko Valley while to the right the water and snow move inexorably toward the Turner Lake chain, to eventually plunge over Hunlen Falls, joining the Atnarko River 11 miles north at the outlet of Lonesome Lake. We named the black peak in front of us Guenevere Mountain, after Camelot's Queen. The sun was getting low and we had a fair distance to go to camp so we left the panoramic viewpoint, returned along the sharp edge, picked up our packs and began the descent.

Due to the shattered outcrops of weak granite, we were obliged to proceed rather slowly once we stepped off the top of the ridge. It was very steep and although the path at first was over small rock and dirt, we were soon down to larger rocks and it became necessary for only one of us to move at a time as we were forced by bluffs to travel nearly straight down and didn't want to risk crashing a rock onto the person below. Finally, after a treacherous 20-minute decline, we

edged carefully between a few last slabs and came to the edge
of the glacier. A creek meandering along over the surface
made it slippery so we decided to follow the moraine. As
Jack stepped between two large rocks resting insecurely on
their ends, one just leaned over an inch or two, enough to
catch his leg tightly by the knee. He couldn't reach the stone
himself, so I set down my can of alpine flowers and came to
his rescue. After this incident we tried the glacier for a bit.
Once we left it, we were on a large barren flat covered with
strange rock formations. We started down with the slope
growing steeper all the time, although the travelling was
fairly easy, being over soft dirt and pebbles. We headed for
a small knoll far below, where we hoped to camp.

Part way down we were confronted with a steep strip of
rock-hard snow about 30 feet wide, packed so firmly we
could not even dig a heel into the surface. It would be very
risky to chance slipping on the snowslide since it was not only
steep in itself, but led to a sheer drop of unknown height,
just 100 feet farther down. The only solution was to
take the axe and cut foot-sized steps in the ice. As Jack was
doing this, chunks rolled down the steep slope, providing an
irresistible challenge for Skye who lunged down the chute in
hot pursuit. Fortunately, her claws were able to dig into the
smooth surface well enough for her to stop when she wanted
to. She'd chase a chunk almost to the breakover, and as it
disappeared over the brink, turn and gallop back up to in-
tercept another one.

Not long after this we hit the first low alpine balsam which
are so thick and low it made walking extremely difficult. We
soon found easier going where there were many flowers of
which asters, arnicas, and Indian paintbrush were the most
prominent. There were many other little, less showy flowers,
moss, grass and the ubiquitous heather. Many small streams
ran down the mountainside, keeping the entire region well
watered.

We just had time to set up camp on the flat, hard-surfaced
promontory and eat supper amidst swarms of starving
mosquitoes before it was dark. Even generous applications of
insect repellent did not deter those mosquitoes one bit. They
crowded onto us so thickly our shirts were black with them.
As soon as we crawled into bed we were forced to seek refuge
under our sleeping bags until the need for air sent us out
where the hordes waited. We eventually solved it by

burrowing under the covers, leaving only a tiny hole close to our noses to breathe through. A few ravenous monsters found the hole, came buzzing in, drills spinning, and proceeded to gorge themselves. I had heard rumors that Arctic mosquitoes use electric drills to probe for blood, but had dismissed it as a tall tale. After surviving the onslaught of their cousins that night, I'm no longer so sure!

The following morning we hiked up near a creek to eat breakfast after which we continued our torturous way through blueberries growing under the pines and the balsam of the drier places while false rhododendron occupied the moister areas. Dense alpine balsam spread their low branches far out from their thick trunks so we actually had to walk on them while hanging on to the branches above. There were places where we simply sat down on the solid carpet of white heather and "ottered" down to a lower level. We emerged at last onto the south rim of the natural amphitheatre we had been heading for the previous evening. Mountain goats had trails down the steep rim to the bottom and we used these whenever they were suitable for less sure-footed creatures such as us. The trip from camp to the basin had taken about three hours, yet we had travelled only three miles. As the sky was steadily gathering black cumulus clouds, we had to quit the alpine country and begin the homeward trek.

After crawling under and climbing over windfall and squeezing ourselves between close-growing pines for several hours, we hit fir and huge aspen. By then we were about half-a-mile south of where our journey had started the day before.

An hour later we were home. Although the sky had threatened rain all afternoon, little fell until a few minutes after we opened the door. Then it poured!

The names of many of the lakes, creeks and rivers which surround us have an interesting history. Some of them are Indian. Tenas, meaning "small" is one of these as is Atnarko which means "clear water" and Hotnarko which translates "black water". The Indian word Talchako means "white water". Turner Lake is named for an early settler who lived down the valley more than half-a-century ago. Lonesome Lake got its name when my father arrived there in January, 1913. When he landed at the north end of the lake in the dead of winter and nothing was stirring, the lake seemed extremely lonely in comparison with the way it had been at first sight the previous August when the valley was alive with waterfowl and other forms of life.

Weather and seasons make a tremendous change in the landscape and is one reason why every trip we embark on is so different from all the others. The days immediately preceding our next expedition were hot and clear but near the end of July the weather turned sour. We had watered the corn, tomatoes and melons, a certain invitation to rain! This time the recreational climb was combined with a scheduled plane trip so our plans were not flexible.

We rose on August 1 at 5 a.m. to get everything shipshape for three weeks. Skye and the hens had been taken to my mother's place as she had agreed to look after them in our absence. Each carrying a pack, we secured the compound on our way so no one could open gates and allow the cow in the field to get out, or cows and horses outside to get in. We then hiked to the Venturi Bridge and started the gentle climb to the mountain base. As we began the real ascent, I kept glancing back, wondering why I wasn't being nudged by Skye, only to remember she was not with us this time. Skye loved such trips and knew perfectly well we were going off when we took her to my mother. I missed her and felt a little guilty going off on a mountain jaunt without her.

Just as we reached the one-third way to the peak, we heard an airplane fly over the valley and scrambled up the back side of a bluff so we could look down on the Edwards place and Big Lagoon. From this vantage point we watched the plane land and taxi to the hangar. In the ensuing silence the tinkle of horse bells floated up to us and we could even hear voices. Pushing onwards we reached the top of the outcrop from which we could overlook Fogswamp Farm. We should also have been able to see the rugged glacier-clad mountains west of Turner Lake and the Talchako River but those majestic peaks looked as though someone had plunked a great gob of whipped cream on each one. We carried on through white bark pine and ripening blue huckleberry bushes. When at last the lodgepole pine gave way to balsam and the ground appeared red with huckleberry leaves, we knew we were close to open going. Higher yet, Lyall's lupine bloomed with bright blue-purple blossoms resembling red clover and were accompanied by red Indian paintbrush. The lupine climbed to the 7,000-foot level together with a few bluebells.

We headed for water. The short yellow grass gave way to

flowers and green grass on horizontal benches about two feet wide and a foot or so high. These have evolved over the centuries as mud sliding downhill during spring runoff, came to a stop to form a slight ridge. Later in the season seeds fell on the moist soil, binding it. Year by year as more soil flows down, it halts against the ridge and builds higher. After many years a bench is formed, complete with lush grass and flowering plants. Everything happens slowly above timberline. A tree takes decades to accomplish even a foot of growth.

It took us just three hours to climb to timberline but it was another half-hour or so before we came to water which flowed sweet and bitingly cold from under thin sheets of ice.

A cliff about 1,000 feet high had large corners of snow clinging to the top of the crumbling wall, which kept splitting off and plunging down into a beautiful blue lake at the base. We gazed down the valley and over the rolling country before slanting down into a lower pass dappled with round, shallow ponds, the largest of which is about 50 feet across, while the smallest are mere puddles, four or five feet across. The lake-filled pass appears solid green from a distance but on walking through it, one discovers marsh marigold, red Indian paintbrush, asters, yellow arnicas, monkshood and a sweet flower resembling a white blooming timothy head.

Two ptarmigan suddenly burst into the air in front of us, whirred away, banked sharply and glided back into the alpine willow again.

Descending into the next basin we were greeted by the mountain ventriloquist, the hoary marmot. We could not see the animal at first but finally sighted him, a black stumplike mass on top of a mound of bare earth, far out in the center of the basin. Then another, down by a stream. Susan spotted a third running across the grass above us. They all whistled from time to time and as we drew closer, slid down their holes and vanished. We detected several of their homesites marked by piles of scat and worn-out looking hay. By living so compactly they had worn trails in the hard soil. We followed a six-inch-wide one along the hillside 100 feet or more.

As we moved eastward, alpine birch covered vast areas, their low crawling branches rising up at the tips like questing heads of snakes. We planned to spend the night on the upper end of a long moraine where we had made an opening in the center of a clump of balsam. We left our packs there and continued on for a foray through the flowers, birch and grass, planning to return to the campsite by dark.

It was cool but not raining as we began exploring. More ptarmigan burst out from the birch practically under our feet. These differed from the white tail ptarmigan on the west side of the mountain which were light and dark gray on their fronts. The eastern ones were a rich mixture of light and dark broken wavy lines of rusty chestnut. Their backs and tails were dark brown, legs white and feathered and their white wings appeared pointed at the tip in flight but in glide position were broad and round-tipped. A white ring around the eye with red patch above made these willow ptarmigan beautiful birds indeed.

Next we came across a pair with several small, downy babies. The parents would not fly because their chicks were so small. Mother and hatchlings came first, then the male rose out of the grass at Jack's feet, clucking and fussing. The female rushed forward in an effort to divert us. As I advanced, both adults started running in a peculiar series of quick steps, paused while they stood high and looked all around, then bobbed down their heads and ran forward again. Their tails continually flicked up and down in time with their running feet and they kept up a constant clucking as they ran in a circle right around where their chicks hid in dense grass!

Before returning to the campsite we rambled to another of the creeks which joins the Hotnarko River and enjoyed the flowers growing there. We could see the 6,000-foot pass we would climb the next morning on our way to Charlotte Lake. As we erected our plastic roof, we noticed fog had cut visibility to under six miles. After heating up and eating some stew and bread, we lay down to try to sleep on what must be the hardest piece of land in the entire province, if not in all Canada! The night wasn't too cold so our light sleeping bags kept us warm enough. Several times through the night of restless sleep we heard ptarmigan seemingly wondering who had taken over their roosting place. No one was the least keen to linger in bed the next morning, so we rose soon after daybreak. Once the fire was going with dead balsam wood and some fir pitch carried up from the valley, we made toast on a fork cut from an alpine birch.

After thoroughly soaking the fire, which was only three feet from the stream, we made up our packs and started off. The clouds were hanging even lower and a cold wind was blowing, but the flowers along our way cheered us. The obscured mountains were a distinct loss, however, and gray clouds scudded low over the pass we were to climb. Above us were huge broken rocks but the ones we walked on had been there for awhile and were covered with black fungi.

Even in this rough part of Trumpeter Mountain the hoary marmot obviously still found food to accompany the excellent homesites provided by the rocks. Some marmot houses are just holes under stones but others are dug out of soil. There are untrampled flowers growing all round the entrances and how the animal gets in and out without crushing them is a mystery. One marmot is always on watch duty on a high rock, sounding a shrill whistle at any sign of danger. Once the alarm has been sounded it takes some time before the marmots gain enough courage to come out of their holes. They are beautiful creatures, rich brown on their faces, bellies, legs and tails. The back is mostly a frosty brown, making them appear to have been out in a light fall of snow. Their paws are black. An adult weighs about 10 pounds and is heavier during the summer than when it comes out of winter hibernation.

Although all the eastern end of the range is rocky and broken, the highest point is a castle-like formation rising to 7,282 feet, contrasting with gentle ridges to the east. As the rocks became predominantly red and purple, fine-grained and broken into square blocks, we came to a place where Jack spied the head and horns of a large mountain goat gazing arrogantly down at us from his rocky perch. We took turns looking at him through the binoculars until he abruptly vanished. Through trees, grass and flowers we descended to an old burn where the trunks of what was once a forest stood everywhere. A new crop of trees is rising to replace them, but it will take time. As we climbed lower, great glacier-worn rocks hunched in our path. We were heading for a particularly large red rock sticking out of a timbered flat, beyond which we expected to find the big meadow we were looking for.

Scrambling over a rotten pine log, Jack was in the lead. A few seconds later, Susan was confronted by the infuriated buzzing of 100 yellowjackets. Apparently Jack had broken into their nest and they emerged boiling mad, ready to attack anything in sight. Susan was just about to step up on the log when she spotted them. I was right behind her and saw them almost simultaneously. We plunged off through the downed timber in different directions so as not to get in each other's way. Miraculously, no one got stung!

By the time we arrived at our destination, we were quite parched, not even having seen water since lunchtime. We tramped through knee-high slough grass and soon came to a slow stream where we enjoyed a drink of cold, good-flavored water. After resting a few minutes, we spotted a medium sized black bear across the far side of the meadow and watched him as he poked along. Once in awhile he turned his head toward us but as we were some distance away and there was no wind, he remained unaware of us. We wanted to get down to the lake shore where there was a trail so we followed a moose track until it ran out, then set off down a small creek before entering a pine grove with trees so tightly packed it was extremely difficult to make progress. They were just skinny little things but covered on all sides with dead branches that seemed designed to rip a passerby's shirt or pack.

On a gravel beach on the north shore of Charlotte Lake we came across a relic of "civilization" in the form of a plastic bleach bottle. Pollution seems to be with us even in the most isolated areas. Way up on Trumpeter Mountain where a survey party built a rock cairn, there are empty cans to mar the wilderness. Where we camped on the moraine, someone had been there long before us, leaving as their memorial some tins to rust among the Scouler's pinks.

We reached a tourist resort on the lake and accepted the hospitality of the kind lodge caretakers. We were even lucky enough to be given a ride to Nimpo Lake the next day. The airport is a mile south of there so we walked in and ate supper by a small stream. We had just begun to make camp when a chorus of coyotes started up. We wanted to see them as they sounded quite close, so walked until we almost reached them but a silly grouse burst out of a tree just then and the coyotes shut up and refused to yip another yap! We continued to stalk them but even when we managed to stir their curiosity by imitating them, we could not get a clear view across the ravine. We thought there were four, but couldn't be certain.

210

After making camp we scraped up pine needles to make a more or less soft, warm mattress, then went down to the lake shore to watch boats humming down its length and disappearing in the dusky distance. After we turned in we heard loons several times. Near morning the doleful bellow of a cow reached us from across the lake.

Our plane was due around noon next morning but hours passed and there was no sign of it, a common enough occurrence in our part of the world! An airstrip can seem desolate as moonscape and to keep warm we paced the entire length of it to see if it met specifications! A truck came along and the driver advised us that sometimes the airline sent a Goose, in which case it would land on the lake. He offered to drive us to the seaplane dock but enroute another truck intercepted us and told us the twin Otter was waiting at the strip.

Once we were aboard, the plane took off in an easterly direction but after gaining altitude, turned west toward the fog and mist-covered Coast Range. It was clear above the Atnarko-Bella Coola valley but most of the higher mountains were hidden.

The pilot landed at Vancouver International Airport two hours late.

17

Fogswamp Horse Sagas

On our farm, as on any other, animals must be depended on to such an extent they become almost members of the family. Anecdotes about one critter or another form the basis for much conversation in our home. Some tales are hilarious while others are tragic.

A horse that assisted me in the early days of Fogswamp's development was Thuja. This mare was bought in 1951 as an unbroken four-year-old. Thuja's initial encounter with the Hotnarko River was when the water was high and it was a dramatic meeting. As she reached the bank of the turgid river she got into such deep water a coffee-colored wave surged right over her rump and back, soaking both of us. Thuja made a prodigious leap straight up the vertical bank and carried both herself and me to safety. This feat gave me the satisfying feeling I had found an exceptionally good horse. Despite the fact she tended to be snappy all her life, the years proved this to be a correct evaluation. Even so, she sometimes seemed determined to do things wrong. Not once but twice she managed to get herself stranded over a log by stopping her jump just as her front feet hit the ground. It nearly cost her life when she got herself hung up in this way while on range. If she had not been needed for work she might have starved to death for there is no way she could have managed to get out of the predicament without help. The same horse also managed to bind herself tightly against a stump on another occasion. She rolled too close to it and ended up lying on her side with her belly against the stump, front legs on one side of it, back legs on the other. Since the ground sloped towards the stump she couldn't manage the necessary leverage to rise. Thuja looked positively embarrassed after being rescued with ropes.

It was Thuja who once tried to get a drink from the floating bridge spanning the river close to the Edwards' place. Apparently she was "sudden took" with thirst and was too impatient to take the long way round to the bank. Impetuously she walked out on the bridge and stepped off onto the leaves and needles banked against it, apparently mistaking this material for part of the bridge. She plunged head first into the water and once more had to be roped to safety!

The tricky job of getting horses on and off a raft for transport on the lake creates all sorts of opportunities for them to get into trouble in a variety of ingenious ways. Thuja distinguished herself during the disembarkment proceedings one time when, instead of stepping off the raft into the water from the side, she elected to depart from the bow. There happened to be two logs projecting off the front of the raft with a crack between them just exactly wide enough to catch and hold a horse's leg, as Thuja managed to prove. She started to leave the raft, lowering her foot into the water as far as possible without putting any of her weight on it. Not feeling bottom, she tried to withdraw her foot. In the process, she inserted it neatly between the two logs. This put her suddenly off balance and she fell sideways. It seemed certain she would have broken her leg, but miraculously she was none the worse for her ridiculous accident.

Despite the fact Thuja was a dependable horse and could carry huge weights on the trickiest trail, she clearly hated coming down hills and always navigated them as though expecting treachery from the rocks under her feet. Thuja was retired to greener pastures when she was 23 years old and stiff in all her limbs. Her horseshoe is tacked up on our verandah, along with those other four-legged homesteaders.

Some of the funniest stories concern Lucky, a 1,500 pound chunk of friendly horseflesh still livening our fields. Lucky once decided it had been an oversight that he was not loaded on the raft. In his attempt to remedy the error, he launched himself into the water even though the raft was pulling well away from the shore. He then tried to rear in nine feet of water and heave himself aboard. He had to be fended off with a pole until he finally took the hint and returned to shore to wait for the second loading.

Horses sometimes seem totally illogical. They will walk on deep water ice without any regard as to whether it is strong enough to hold them...sometimes. The very same animal will revolt against being led across a shallow frozen ditch. Lucky becomes a trembling "booby" on the raft at times and once created quite a problem by displaying intense fear of a bridge. This occurred when Lucky was first being brought home and, in fact, earned him his name.

A half-hour had been spent futilely trying to persuade the stubborn horse to cross a wooden bridge. Eventually he was blindfolded with a sack. Still protesting and ricocheting from side to side in panic, he was led across the planking which, to his obvious amazement, held his weight. In the course of the remainder of the trip home there were several more bridges to be crossed. Each was in worse condition than the first, but he went over these with no fuss at all, even trying to walk on flimsy poles placed across small streams. This horse made so much trouble for himself on the way to his new home, tangling his feet in brush and sticking several sharp branches into his belly, the consensus was he was Lucky to get there!

Since by 1962 the flock of trumpeter swans had increased to 250 birds and the amount of grain required was 9,000 pounds, obtaining a third horse was necessary. Following a trip to Vancouver in the summer we stopped at Anahim Lake and bought a completely unbroken black mare, six or seven years old. After halter breaking her so she could be led in to Stillwater, she was turned loose there with Rommy and Thuja. This precipitated a big fight in which the new horse was trounced and driven out of the pasture. When we came to collect the horses some time later, we found the two senior ones easily enough but the new horse, Rocket, was not with them. By following her tracks we located her about half-a-mile away, trying to hide under a clump of birch trees. Finding her was easy. Catching her was something else again! We couldn't get nearer than about 30 feet before she would wheel and flee, finally rocketing up a steep-sided draw with her hopeful captors in hot pursuit. Jack was carrying three-year-old Susan on his back but still managed to climb about as fast as the neurotic horse. The higher Rocket climbed the worse the going became. In the end, the horse was fenced in by huge boulders and brought to bay in a box canyon. Even with Jack blocking the only exit she would not allow anyone close enough to put a rope on her, turning and threatening to kick whoever tried. Eventually a rope snare was set and she walked out and caught herself. Once captured, Rocket behaved in quite a civilized manner. Still, none of us was at all certain how the frisky horse would react to the prospect of crossing Stillwater on a raft.

Rommy and Thuja were taken over first. Returning across the river for Rocket, I led her up to the raft where the bow was grounded. After smelling at it for only a moment, Rocket stepped right on as though she had been travelling that way for years. She stood quietly, head hanging over the tie rail and remained calm all the way across the river. On Lonesome Lake, Rocket took her place on the big raft, with a cow and the two other horses. She once again stood quietly, not even appearing to mind the noise of the outboard motor. As the water was high the raft was taken up the river at the head of Lonesome Lake. It happened that just as we passed Big Lagoon, an airplane took off and flew low over the heads of the horses with a mighty roar. Rocket just glanced casually at it and went back to resting her chin on the tie rail.

Despite her placid acceptance of these unusual occurrences, the same horse manged to catch her thick black tail on a loose branch and instantly went berserk! She tore through the woods, her branch-tangled tail streaming out behind her. After several minutes of violent effort, the branch fell off and she calmed down. Rocket remains hard to catch but has improved considerably. She likes oats so is no trouble on the packing job. She will frequently refuse to be caught out in the field but will willingly follow the other horses to the barn, then stand and permit herself to be caught. Her attitude seems to be: "I can bloody well walk in on my own four legs and you puny humans can catch me when I allow you to."

Rocket is an extremely intelligent horse. One day I went to put her in the barn for supper, but she declined to be approached closer than about 10 feet. I simply closed the barn door and strode to the house. With an expression of disbelief on her face, Rocket watched me go. She whinnied hopefully but when no one went back to the barn to let her in, she walked purposefully down to the house and pushed her nose against one of the windows. To prevent the window being broken, I took a halter and went outside, planning to at least drive her away from the glass. As soon as I was in view, the smart horse left the window of her own accord and walked right up to me, thrusting her head into the halter. She was, of course, rewarded by being put into the barn where her hay was, but that time it was on my terms, not hers!

Rocket gave us some chuckles on another occasion. She and two other horses were being fed in a corral during a packing trip. I threw them part of a bale of hay which happened to be little better than humus. Being boss of that particular trio of equines, Rocket immediately pre-empted the hay only to discover as she tore the quarter bale apart that the more she examined it, the worse the hay seemed to be. After scattering several layers around in the muck, she tossed a chunk of it to one of her companions, as if to say, "Eat it, Guenevere, it's good enough for *you,*" Rocket then stamped around on what was left, finishing up by urinating on top of it before turning to look me straight in the eye, clearly demanding a better deal. Susan and I had a good laugh over the performance before providing the horses with a bale of acceptable quality.

Rocket also entered the annals of horse-laughs when she was being taken across an iced-over channel about 10 feet wide. Instead of using the trail Jack had chopped out after he realized the ice was thin in the middle, Rocket elected to use the ice. When it broke, she slipped, ending up with her rump half-way under the ice. After struggling in the mud and frozen chunks, she managed to rise—much colder, wetter and, possibly, a little wiser.

To this day Rocket finds it difficult to accept with equanimity the prospect of having a rider on her back. She tenses up and obviously would prefer not to have anyone touch her. The only exception to this is during fly season when she will voluntarily rub her head against someone to ease the torment of the little black flies which crawl into her ears. She will take the bit into her mouth herself rather than have anyone touch her chin. She takes no exception to a pack, saddle or harness, as these are inanimate.

An attempt was once made to train her to be ridden and I

led her around with Jack on her back. After half-an-hour or so, the lead rope was removed and Jack was on his own or rather, Rocket was. All went well for about 100 feet, then the mare seemed to realize what had happened. She reared a couple of times and began to buck. As Jack was bareback, it was not long before he went sailing over the horse's head to land spreadeagled in a couple of feet of snow. The triumphant horse trotted off to the barn, her tail proudly bannered, head high and mane flying. Jack was unhurt, but had left a man-sized impression in the snow. Obviously, Rocket couldn't be left with her victory. We set off to catch her and loaded about 260 pounds of sacked stuff on her back but being an excellent packhorse, she made no trouble about that at all. Rocket eventually learned to tolerate a rider but remains tense about it and no one knows exactly what she will do if a heel tickles her sides.

A further increase in swans and the loss of Rommy in 1968 meant two more horses were required. In Hagensborg we soon lined up a thoroughly pampered long-legged five- or six-year-old bay mare. Not wanting to make a special trip into Anahim Lake for just one horse, we decided to look around and see if we couldn't locate the second one we needed at the same time. Sure enough, we discovered a short, extremely splay-footed, totally spoiled four-year-old fawn-colored gelding. His right leg was deformed but we were told the left one had already been cured by the use of a half shoe to straighten the fetlock and the right one would doubtless respond similarly. We were also assured that he was just a young horse, three years old at the most, which would indicate his bones were still somewhat flexible.

Fogswamp would soon become home for Guenevere and Spud. Guenevere after the queen in Camelot and Spud simply because the name suited him. But first there was the task of getting them home. Both horses were trucked separately as far as possible. From that point on they would have to make their way home on foot with us.

It was the first time Guenevere had ever been away from where she had been raised and she was so distraught she trembled and shook with terror. She quaked even more when taken to a creek to drink. Obviously, she was scared to death of water. When I tried to lead her across a creek she first refused completely, then gathered herself together and

218

made a flying leap, nearly clearing the whole ten-foot stream. She still has the same enthusiasm when crossing a creek and would prefer to leave it as a dim memory behind her.

She used to try to leave the raft in much the same manner, a tendency which had to be discouraged for her own sake as well as that of any humans around! She has gradually learned to disembark with a degree of decorum, at least as long as someone keeps a good hold on her head.

Guenevere calmed down when the gelding arrived to accompany her on the trip to Fogswamp. Since both horses had been living alone, they were lonely and became good friends right away. The first time water was encountered on the trail, Guenevere flatly refused to put her feet into it. The stream was only a few inches deep but too wide for even her to jump. Jack was leading her but just couldn't persuade Guenevere to get her feet wet. If it hadn't been for Spud, the mare might be there yet! He was led around her and splashed nonchalantly across as though he had been doing it all his life. When Guenevere saw Spud heading away from her, she gathered all her courage and plodded bravely into the gravel-bed stream which barely covered her hooves.

The next stretch of water was another matter entirely. In late April the Hotnarko River is in full flood, coffee-colored and fast-moving. It is about 60 feet wide at the place the horses were to cross. Spud went first, on a rope thrown across the river. No trouble. As soon as he had reached the other side, Guenevere went crazy, pawing great holes in the ground, whinnying hysterically and lunging frantically around the tree she was tied to. When it came her turn she was willing enough to follow her friend but instead of walking across as Spud had done, she made one of her colossal leaps and landed with a huge brown splash about 10 feet out in the river. She walked the rest of the way!

So, with Spud placidly leading the way and Guenevere making wild leaps across the smallest trickles, the party made its erratic way to the head of Lonesome Lake.

Later that spring when Jack was bringing the horses from pasture, Guenevere jumped a creek with her usual enthusiasm. In the process, she managed to ram Jack so hard he went down on a sharp rock and was hurt. This so enraged me I grabbed the mare's rope and took her across the creek, snubbing her hard each time she tried to clear it until she got the idea, and walked across. All the 15 miles home, Guenevere got the "treatment" every time we came to a stream. She would still rather jump than walk, but she walks!

The next job was to train the horses to pack and both of them took to it with little difficulty, carrying two 100-pound sacks of soil round to get them used to heavy weights. They worked well on the real packing job, too, although Guenevere won herself a whopping when she lay down in a pile of sand a couple of times. Part of the problem lay in the fact that Guenevere is a fast walker and often had time to get restless and mischievous while the other horses were catching up to her.

Spud and Guenevere worked together all spring but the results were not spectacularly great, Spud could think of a lot of things he would rather do than pull heavy loads. When they were put to the task of hauling a load of logs one horse alone could have pulled easily, Spud would start with the mare all right but if the load didn't move right away, he would fade out. When I punished him, he kicked at me, which earned him a hot rump. Both horses jack-knifed at every opportunity and got all tangled up. The real moment of truth arrived when haying started. Spud tried to kick the tongue off the rake whenever a turn was made with him on the inside. But of the pair, it was Guenevere who hated the rig most. She didn't like any machinery but her rage boiled over when she was hitched to the hay rake. She'd chomp her bit, great gobs of foam flying like whipped cream from her lips. She would bite the neck yoke or martingale, prance, stop, back up, rear and rush forward with her head down and her neck as stiff as a bar of iron. I spanked her when she acted up but this only resulted in her becoming increasingly frustrated and angry. She sweated so much she became soaking wet, water streaming off her body like rain off a roof. The entire project was not good for woman, beast or the machinery! The work wasn't getting done, either.

Later in the haying season, quite by accident, I discovered a way to by-pass some of the anger. By making Guenevere stop frequently before she got too wrought up, things went much more smoothly.

Guenevere is a great pack horse who will accept just about any load. Early in her career, she even managed the 10-gallon drums of gas and kerosene oil without too much trouble, except for trying to bulldoze a few rocks and trees off the trail with the drums. The containers were partially empty as a result of having some of the contents used on the job. This made a lot of space for the kerosene to slop around in. When the horse went downhill, the fluid would all rush to the front ends of the drums with a slurp. As soon as she started to climb out of the hollow, it all rushed to the other end with another loud slurp. The movement of the contents of the drums would cause the end of the containers to bang. Slurp... bang... slurp... bang! Even the first time this occurred, Guenevere didn't so much as turn one of her ridiculously long ears backward towards the noise but just plodded along with a slightly skeptical expression on her long face as she studiously ignored the racket.

What Guenevere really lives for, though, is to run. She would rather run with a rider on her back, than eat. One January day she was racing so hard with me on her that with a temperature of 16°F and at a speed of about 30 miles an hour, some of my skin actually froze under three layers of warm clothing.

Spud spent the early part of his life disliking work. Part of this may have been because of his splayed right foot. It turned out he was a mature four-year-old and the crooked leg did not improve with age. He managed to pack well and had a great personality but he was always lazy. One day Spud was standing under a couple of cedars where a swing had been put up for Susan. Noticing he had not moved for an unusually long time, even for Spud, I went to investigate and discovered the horse had lifted his left front leg up and shoved it through the swing. When he tried to walk away, he discovered he was caught. Being of a phlegmatic temperament, he just calmly waited until the rescue he knew would come, arrived. It was a simple matter for me to lift the leg but it was something he couldn't do for himself as each time he tried, his hoof brought the swing with him.

Despite the stupidity horses seem to display every so often, there are times when they really exhibit "horse sense". On a pack trip from Stillwater to Lonesome Lake one windy morning, Jack removed the covering from the freight pile, preparatory to loading. The 40-mile gale snatched the huge sheet of black plastic right out of his hands and wrapped it around Rommy. Although he was completely encased in the stuff, the horse just stood still while Jack hauled it all off him. Rommy then gazed at the black crinkly monster as though wondering why Jack would allow it to attack him in such a manner.

When Rommy grew old Susan liked to ride him around. He was 24 at the time she started to ride solo and somewhat thinner than when he was younger, with a sway back and a pot belly. He had always been a sweet-tempered horse and easy to catch. Rommy carried his packs well, although occasionally he attempted to move some of the trees back from the trail with his pack. When crossing a stream he sloshed through it, throwing up a huge shower in front of himself, generally spraying the person leading him. Coming down rockslide trails he insisted on raising his head so high he couldn't possibly see where to put his feet, so tended to proceed with extreme slowness, provoking the person leading him to pull on the rope. This only made him lift his head even higher. Eventually he arrived at the bottom and his head resumed its normal position as he shuffled his lazy way along the trail again. Even so, in the last year of his life he packed a load very little lighter than that of the youngest horses.

Horse behavior on the pack trail can be both amusing and annoying. Most of the amusement occurs years later when the story is being recalled in the safe comfort of our warm kitchen!

Horses are never tied together when negotiating the tricky trails. It is safer for all concerned if each horse has only itself to worry about. Therefore they are all lined up on separate leads with the person in front holding all of them. If a horse stumbles he can be given time to regain balance. This, of course, involves stopping all the horses which must then be pulled to get the pack-train moving again. All of this necessitates a lot of exertion and shortens tempers as the day wears on. Most of the stops and starts are on grades which the horses seem to feel they have all the time in the world to negotiate.

Occasionally a horse will react to a frightening situation with surprising calm just when they might be forgiven for panicking. Susan and I were taking five horses along a little used trail with me on Guenevere and Susan on Thuja. As

222

Guenevere passed under a large tree, a 10-foot section of dead birch fell off, striking horse and rider. I instinctively mumbled "whoa" as I passed out. When I came to a few seconds later, I realized the horse had not moved so much as a hoof after the accident. The huge branch had fallen about three feet onto my head and shoulder, hit Guenevere's rump and crashed to the ground by the horse's feet. With a thundering headache and a fancy lump on my head, I went home, very thankful the horse had not made a bad situation worse by running and throwing me.

There is a younger horse at Fogswamp now, completing the quartet of which Guenevere, Lucky and Rocket are the senior members. In 1975 on our way home from a trip, we came through the Chilcotin and, enroute, purchased a yearling filly we named Cloud. She is white, with dark lower legs, ear tips, tail and lower mane. Being part Arab, she has prominent lustrous dark eyes. Cloud was bought to eventually replace Rocket who is now somewhere in her twenties, still fat and hard to catch but doing her work satisfactorily.

It's not only horses that provide colorful material for stories around our kitchen table. Sometimes the cows on the place pull a few tricks as well. It is unbelievable the number of things that can go wrong when one is trying to produce a bit of milk and cream. I am convinced that if large ranches had only a quarter of our troubles, they would all go broke!

18

Cow Problems and Problem Cows

It is a good policy to keep two cows in order to have milk the year round. A cow shouldn't milk a full year and then have another calf without a rest period of at least two months before the next lactation period. The second cow takes over the milk supplying job while the other cow rests, or that's the theory. Things don't always work out according to plan, however.

The cow we were milking when Jack and I got married failed to become pregnant for two years so we had just one for milk during that time. Wishing to increase the herd a little, we bought a young cow from the Edwards which in turn presented us with a heifer calf on Christmas Day, 1958. Shortly after that, we went to Vancouver for Susan's arrival. In our absence, my parents looked after the stock and when we returned March 16, the cows were brought home. A few days later the cow we had bought found and ate a small amount of poison parsnip, a common and extremely toxic weed of swamps in the area. She was in terrible agony and as we knew of no cure, Jack shot her.

Upi, our milker, calved a few days later but managed to walk over a low stump and rip a triangular hole in her udder. I snipped off the loose flap to prevent infection and it healed satisfactorily.

That same year Upi's 16-month-old heifer named Apple gave birth to a small heifer calf that could not stand up. It was premature but, more than that, there was something wrong with her legs. She was given some time to see if she would be able to overcome the condition but as a trip to Vancouver was in the offing and no one would be around to help her suck her mother, it was reluctantly decided she would have to be shot or she would starve to death.

After we got home, Apple bawled and searched for her baby calf where she had last seen it the day I killed it. She looked straight at me and seemed to be asking where her little one was. It was a shattering experience.

This is an ugly side to farming I will never get used to. Even the necessary butchering of an animal to provide meat is an agonizing business. Living as we do with the farm animals as close companions makes it a very personal business. It was even harder when Susan was little and couldn't comprehend the necessity of killing a "friend".

Apple still had something in her udder and seemed to want to be milked so I cooperated, feeling very sorry and thinking it was the least I could do. In about a week Apple was producing 10 to 12 pounds of milk a day although she was only 17 months old and had not been milked for more than three weeks. The next calf Apple had was lost on the range south of Elbow Lake when he was only five or six months old. We were on a packing trip at the time and figure a predator probably got him.

Domino, the Hereford bull, was acquired in 1962. All our calves are Ayrshire-Hereford cross, not too good a mixture if one wants milk, but a fine combination if meat is desired.

One of Upi's heifers named Friendship proved rather a poor producer, aborting half the time so she had to be bred again. As a result her calves came four months or more later than they were planned for. In 1967 she was supposed to calve in April but didn't make it until July, when she produced a well-built little heifer calf we named Nimue whose life nearly ended just nine days later.

She was tied on a chain 400 feet from the house where there is pasture. It was necessary to milk Friendship at regular intervals to help avoid udder troubles, so the calf was separated from her by one of the eight-foot deer gates. Nimue could get to the gate but not to the cow. At this time both Apple and Friendship were in the pasture which has a small muddy pond in the center and a bridge over the drainage stream for the cows to cross on. When Susan and I went up to the pasture to milk one day, both cows stood at the gate and Friendship seemed unusually concerned about her calf. When we got close enough, we saw something had bitten Nimue's back. She was looking extremely miserable and Friendship was covered with water and dirt from crossing the pond, not having taken time to cross on the bridge. It appeared she had thrown dirt all over her back in her rage at the beast assaulting her calf. The ground was all torn up on both sides of the gate which had nearly been pushed over by the frantic mother in her attempts to get to the calf and its attacker.

None of these details registered at first, only that the calf was badly injured. There was very little blood on her as the cow had forced her head between the close rails of the gate and licked the wounds clean. At first it was thought we would have to dispatch Nimue as the injuries covered a large area on the top of her back, right down into the back muscle. It was astounding she was able to stand, but she could even walk a little. Susan went to the house to tell Jack to come with a gun but when he got there, we talked it over and decided to give the heifer a chance to live.

We undid Nimue's chain and carried her to the house, putting her down just outside the yard gate. She was hungry and wanted to suck her mother but this posed a new problem as the holes in her mangled back would press against her mother's dirty flank, so I held Nimue while she nursed. Jack got hot water and boiled needles for the out-of-date penicillin we had on hand and which was injected when she finished nursing. Tranquilizer was administered to alleviate her obvious pain. Friendship stood outside the fence and watched. After the penicillin was injected into the calf's shoulder muscle, all the torn shreds and connecting strips of skin were trimmed to allow better drainage. Nimue was lying down and unable to feel anything so we were able to work on her without difficulty. As a finishing precaution, iodine was poured into every hole and scratch on her body. So much iodine was applied to the calf her skin smelled of it for months afterward! Sulpha ointment was applied later. A shelter was rigged over her and she remained there until she came to about 10 hours later.

We tried to figure what had chewed her and why it hadn't finished her off. The tooth and claw marks indicated a small bear of some kind and Skye had growled in a very serious manner when we had first gone up there. After examining the fence rails carefully, I found some black bear hairs stuck on the bark of the poles. We assumed the bear came along the fence and caught Nimue after some trouble as the wee calf must have run as much as her chain allowed her to, then she would have bellowed with pain and fright when she was lifted up by her back. Friendship would have heard her and come on a gallop, splashing across the pond in her rush. Her anger when she got to the gate must have been positively terrifying. The attacker doubtless got scared by Friendship, tried to carry Nimue off outside the fence so he could eat her in a safer place, but was prevented from doing so by the chain. When the calf was ripped from his teeth, he must have kept going.

Nimue had been flat on her side for 10 hours before she roused, started licking her lips and, without any assistance, slowly got to her feet. We steered Nimue through the gate and she was able to have her supper. We kept her in the yard for two months and after the first week she ran and jumped as though there was little the matter with her although if it was warm, she'd pant hard with her mouth open and lie down from sunrise until the air cooled in the evening.

A young calf's pulse should be no more than 70 but Nimue's was double that the day she was mangled. Three days later it rose to 200, almost too fast to count. It was such a strong pulse that when she was lying on her side, it shook her whole body. After about two weeks it slowed to an almost normal rate.

For the first month we spent three hours each day cleaning and fixing her up. We built a set of stocks to hold her steady while dressing her wounds. Three times each day she was held while she sucked. Then I made a place in the picket fence where she could put her head through and nurse Friendship without getting her wounds contaminated. I pushed the cow into position on her side of the fence and tied her there each day for a week by which time she started doing it on her own volition. Whenever the cow felt like feeding her calf, she lined herself up beside the hole in the fence. As soon as Nimue saw her there, she came galloping to push her head through and feed.

By the time we had to begin the packing job, most of the holes had healed except for the big one on her right shoulder blade which remained open all the time we were gone because her conscientious mother licked the scabs off as fast as they formed.

A few days after Nimue was attacked, Susan saw a small black bear walking along the fence near the field where the cattle were. As we had another bigger calf tied on a chain, Jack shot the bear. The teeth fitted perfectly the holes in Nimue's back and since there are very few black bears around here during the summer, there is an excellent chance we got the culprit.

When Friendship delivered Nimue she had been four months late. In 1968 she aborted, then didn't conceive after three services by Domino so, as we could not afford to maintain and feed an unproductive cow, she was turned into beef late in 1969.

Apple, our other cow, was far along in her pregnancy when we were clearing trail one spring. We were making slow progress as the day was hot and the cow heavy. We had put the universal saddle on another cow with our camp gear loaded on it in order to keep our hands free for the clearing job. Sky had her pack of gas and oil. The "universal saddle", incidentally, is a small, light packsaddle without crosstrees. Three-inch-wide rawhide straps hold the pontoons together over the animal's back and strings tie the pack on. Of course there is a cinch and pad but the whole outfit is exceptionally light and will fit any back from the broadest horse to the peakedest old cow.

We arrived home with the animals late in the afternoon, turned the cows into the pasture overnight and next morning took them back to the head of Tenas Lake where there was plenty of fine feed. Since Apple was not due to freshen until late June, there was no need to keep a close watch, or so we thought.

A few days later, after covering all the tender plants as usual for a three-day trip, we went out to Stuie for the mail. Returning, we met the cows outside one of the gates but as we were hungry, tired and anxious to uncover the garden, we passed right by without paying too much attention except I mentally noted Apple's udder was very large and I figured she might calve early.

The following day we could hear Apple bawling strangely. The first thought was of poison parsnips as she was standing outside the fence, sort of hunched up. I called Jack to get a gun and a can of power saw oil which we had heard could be used to save a cow if she had not already gone down. I ran across the field to the cow, about 100 feet away. When I came close to the fence, I quickly discovered the cause of the lament. Apple had calved three weeks prematurely.

The little heifer was unable to suck the udder as it was too close to the ground for any calf to find it. Newborn calves always turn their mouths up, since the "natural cow's" bag is small and high. The poor little babies of dairy cows must be taught by humans to reach down to the ground to get that all-important first meal. Apple had apparently calved the day before, sometime after we had passed her on the way home. Since her baby had not yet had a thing to eat, Apple was calling to us for help.

The little mite of a heifer was crumpled against the black log but was alive and hungry. She had travelled a distance of almost 200 feet from where she was born, somehow blundering over a rocky trail where there were several logs to negotiate. It was quite a feat for a creature which should have been in an amniotic lake inside its mother for another 21 days. I picked her up in my arms—she weighed only about 50 pounds—and carried her back to the gate near where she was born. While Jack went to the barn for ropes, a milk pail and a small pot, I worked at trying to get the calf to nurse but it seemed she was too tired and weak from not having any food for about 24 hours. After milking out a small amount of milk into the pot and wetting my fingers in the warm liquid, thrusting them into the calf's mouth a few times, I was able to get the calf to suck my fingers. Then her tiny red nose was guided to the pot of milk. She sucked a few swallows before jerking loose and questing for a bag. She was lying down so no one had to hold her. It was just a matter of persisting in getting her to latch onto the milky fingers then following them to the milk. She would suck only a few seconds, then jerk her head up, spraying milk all over me. Each time, a little milk managed to slip down her throat and that was the important thing.

Apple and Early, her calf, were brought into the field and Apple was tied on a picket line so I could observe if she lost the afterbirth she had retained due to the early delivery. If it did not come away in another day, I knew it would be a serious situation. Another day went by, with no sign of it.

Both of them were moved to Bear Island which at that

time was good clover pasture and there is a set of stocks for restraining animals needing medical treatment. Apple was fastened in them and given a shot of penicillin in the shoulder muscle. That evening she was very sick and started shaking from fever produced by infection from the spoiling placenta. She seemed to grow thinner by the hour and her eyes sank into their sockets until the right one almost closed. A blanket was put on her to keep her warm and dry. Early was inside a chicken wire enclosure with low enough sides that Apple could reach in and lick her calf if she wanted to although she didn't seem inclined to do much but hide under spruce trees day and night. After 48 hours she could be given a second shot of penicillin. I got up at three in the morning and just stood beside the cow's trembling body, stroking her neck, not really expecting to see her alive in the morning.

The tough old cow was not only alive but slightly better the following day. She had wandered down to Early and was there when Jack and I went to see her at seven.

The skin on the outside surfaces of all four teats and her nose then turned bright red as if sunburned and the calf's nose turned the same color. The reddened skin grew thick and slowly started to peel. Great slabs came off Apple's nose as the new skin formed underneath. When the teats peeled the new tender skin cracked and became bloody and painful when she was milked or the calf suckled.

It took about a month for her to lose the placenta and in all that time she ate very little grass each day. At times she could be tempted with vegetables or hay but then she would refuse them again for a time. Then she began to consume a small amount of 16 percent dairy feed although the only things she ate in large amounts were bonemeal and limestone. For awhile she was eating about a pound of the two minerals each day. She very likely would have died had her calf not needed her. She must have been existing on duty alone for a good deal of that month. There was no rapid improvement in her health even after she got rid of the afterbirth but she came along slowly, even continuing to produce milk until forced to dry off so she could gain strength over the winter. By late February she was again in condition to try the hazards of bearing a calf. In December, 1969 she gave birth to a 90-pound bull calf one week overdue. We called him Apollo.

Upi, Apple's mother, was such an excellent milk producer

231

that if she calved during winter she became afflicted with ketosis, a sort of debt situation in the body caused by the cow using more energy making milk than it is taking in. This causes the appetite to lag, accentuating the condition to such an extent the cow begins to look like a perabulating rail fence and almost dries off. This decreased production generally results in the cow's body regaining its balance on its own, although the condition can be fatal. In Upi's case she became so thin and weak she wavered when she walked, could hardly bawl, yet she survived. The next time a cow calved in winter, we were prepared with a chemical—sodium propionate—and dispensed some of it each day. This alleviated the condition and so when Apple calved there were 300 pounds of dairy feed on hand for her in hopes it would help. She refused to eat it or anything else, so was put on a once-a-day milking program to lower her milk production. This worked, although she still gave enough milk for her growing calf and for us to have all we needed. We would prefer not to buy and pack in fancy feed or to have the cows produce more milk than we need. A cow freshening on grass doesn't have any trouble of this kind as she willingly eats enough grass to keep her system operating properly and fresh grass has a higher sugar-energy content.

The tale of cows at Fogswamp is rather a dismal one. In the same period of time the Edwards had no great problems despite the fact both families' cows are related and the same bull sired all the calves each year.

Domino has been the herd sire for the past 13 years and every single calf has looked like a Hereford, even though all the mothers except Friendship were Ayshires. Domino is a polled Hereford, yet only half of the calves are polled. Of the three calves Friendship produced, two had horns. Nimue took three months for hers to start to develop but when she was butchered at 18 months, she had quite respectable ones. Nimue couldn't be kept for there was only a limited amount of hay and most of it had to go to the horses.

In addition to being just plain difficult to raise and causing many worries with their illnesses and problem births, the cows have given us a few laughs along the way as well.

A recalcitrant cow will sometimes pretend inability to jump a ditch and will swing her stern end around until she is standing parallel to it. Then, when her head is tugged, she will throw herself at the ditch and fall in. This is, of course, supposed to demonstrate the jump was too much for her, despite the tracks on both sides of the gully which prove otherwise.

One young calf proved to be a ridiculous creature of habit. Since the calf milks the cow while we are away, the young calves on our farm continue to receive their milk directly, eliminating the unpleasant job of teaching the calf to drink from a pail. In the narrow stall where the mother cow was kept, the calf in this story could only negotiate himself in beside her by entering the slot backwards. This procedure was carried on for a couple of months before I became curious as to whether the calf would be capable of finding his breakfast if Mama were in a different place. One morning Susan and I let the cow out prior to opening the calf's stall. As soon as the calf was free, the little fellow headed for the empty stall, where he backed in as usual. Not finding breakfast in the accustomed location, he rushed up the corridor to the open door and despite the fact his mother was mooing encouragingly to him just beyond it, he promptly reversed down the corridor again. When he hit the gate at the bottom, he had to stop. His bewilderment at not finding his mother's milk bag at the end of this reverse trip was amusingly evident. I dragged him out the door to his distraught mother. The same thing happened all over again the following day until it occurred to him that perhaps breakfast was a *cow* rather than a *place*.

Domino, the Fogswamp bull, is also a creature of routine. During winters in the barn he always had the same stall and, when being turned out, always hears the announcement, "Bull out". That is his signal to lumber down to the river for a drink. When it is time for him to return, the words "Bull in" result in his docile return to his own stall. These calls were given in the first place only to alert Susan, when she was younger, that the bull was about to be set loose but Domino knew what the words meant, all right.

Near the end of the barn corridor a gate closes the horse section off from the cattle section. The gate is supposed to be closed when the bull goes in but one day someone forgot and left it swung open against Domino's stall. That evening, when the bull was turned in, he tromped down the hall as usual but when he tried to make the right turn into his stall, he couldn't, so blundered on into the horse area. Poor Domino was decidedly confused and very upset at not finding his stall in its accustomed place. All I could think of was to give the command: "Bull out". The one-ton monster then turned about face and with great dignity lumbered all the way out of the barn to the fence. I then slammed the gate out of the way and announced "Bull in," whereupon the placid bull re-entered the barn and made his way to his stall without difficulty! Domino still holds gentle reign over his three cows on Fogswamp Farm.

These are Valerian and her two daughters. Valerian is a charming black and white cow, a producer of delicious milk. She is unrelated to any of the cows previously described, being the offspring of one named Cinderella which we bought in Hagensborg in 1972. This cow was purchased after Apple was butchered and Domino, left without female company, was depressed!

Cinderella was another accident-prone cow which was attacked by a predator while on range in the spring of 1975. She had been skittish since her earliest days and only through persistence and socializing did she become even slightly trusting. Due to a feed shortage, it was decided to put Cinderella, Domino and a yearling heifer out to pasture. When we went to collect them, the pregnant Cinderella was discovered in dreadful shape, having been clawed and bitten. Ultimately, she had to be shot, her unborn calf dying with her.

Her first offspring, Valerian, is a real clown. One day as I was preparing her for milking, she reached down, grabbed my milk stool and flung it several feet away. She then stood there, looking absolutely innocent as if nothing whatever had happened, or at least, nothing *she* had anything to do with.

Another day she got in the yard when Jack left a gate open. We were working in the garden at the time so Valerian was aware she had only a limited time to do all the mischief she had in mind to accomplish in the place she knew perfectly well she shouldn't be! First she sampled several apples from the lower branches of one of our best trees. She then hurried off and devoured a pail of pea pods and corn husks. Passing a window-box full of flowers she tasted several carnations before sweeping on to eat a small cabbage and several gladiolus growing in a bed by the end of the window. Just as she was finishing, Jack entered the yard and Valerian quickly decided she'd best get into the field again, so she scooted out under the branches of another fruit tree!

Valerian may be a buffoon but like some of the other cows on the place, she has been broken to do light work. During the fall of '74 she hauled in windbreak material. This consists of treetops which are stuck into the ground to protect the young fruit trees from heavy winds.

Valerian has had two calves. One is Don, whose full name is Meridon, born October, 1974, while the littlest one is called Vandemar and was born December, 1975. Both heifers got their names from the letters contained in Valerian and Domino. Don has the most comical face imaginable. Big dark patches across her eyes give her the appearance of a cow in clown makeup.

Because of animal-feeding schedules, we refuse to "spring forward, fall back", timewise as the rest of the country does. It is easier for us to remain on a steady routine and, besides, it takes only a few months before every one realizes we have been right all along!

Even the hens on our farm show a marked ability to create complications where none need to be! Since the henhouse is 30 feet from the barn, I generally tramp out a trail for the feathered creatures when the snow gets deep, to enable them to reach the barn without getting their belly feathers wet. The independent Leghorns rarely take advantage of my thoughtfulness. They impatiently peer out the door and appear to take deep breaths before plunging off through the snow on four separate paths! When it is time for the return trip they each add a new set of tracks on their way to the henhouse. Occasionally they try to fly the distance. With tremendous effort they can manage to get perhaps half-way before losing lift and stalling into the fluffy white snow, floundering and churning the rest of the distance. A particularly smart hen will now and then launch herself from the top of the manure heap and thus make it almost to the door before flopping ignomiously into the cold white stuff. The rare, intelligent hen will use my Trudy-trail.

Not only domestic animals cause problems for themselves. A deer trying to cross the river one day was startled by Jack and leaped blindly into the water, wading and swimming to the opposite bank. Where the doe touched shore, however, the bank is a 10-foot vertical bluff. In her desperation, she tried to jump straight up out of the water onto the high ledge but each leap resulted in her becoming overbalanced just as she almost reached the top. She would fall backwards into the water, throwing up a huge spray.

After several unsuccessful attempts, the doe concluded the jump was too high but, instead of moving upstream to where there is a beach, she charged back across the river to a long sand bar with a 40-foot cottonwood log on it. The frightened deer approached the log midway along its length and tried to scramble over. She was tired and had to rest often as she worked her body over the obstacle. She got over, finally, and still going in a straight line, raced up the beach and crossed the river successfully, vanishing into the bush.

During the building of the "Skuzie trail" which leads from the farm to the summer range at Elbow Lake, our border collie Skye proved herself. The assistance she gave, together with the fact Susan did her part by carrying lunches, gave the trail its composite name. Skye's part in the venture was to carry gas for the small McCulloch saw which is a light, direct drive saw with a shorter bar than the one Jack presented to me as an engagement token. The "Lady Mac" has a small fuel tank so needs frequent refueling. I thought up the idea of training the dog to carry gas so it would always be handy.

At first Skye gave the distinct impression that being a pack animal was not the way a *sheep* dog should earn its keep and she sulked when shown the saddle. This was just a piece of cowhide bent over the dog's back and tied across her chest with one string while another was cinched under her belly to ensure the load would not slip over her head when she leaned down to drink. Cowhide boxes large enough to carry two quart cans were laced on each side, with sacking fastened over the top. I ignored Skye's disgust and put the saddle on, telling her all the time what a good and useful dog she was to help with the trail building. After about three sessions of this kind of propaganda, Skye became sold on the idea she was doing a pretty important piece of business and would come to the pack, tail wagging, ready to push her head into the harness. She carried the pack whenever we were travelling on a trail and even though the amount she carried was small, it was a help.

The dog quickly learned the meaning of the urgent yell "gas" and would run to where Jack was working but she had to be taught to stay away from the saw when it was running. For some reason she didn't seem to have any natural fear of the slashing chain saw whipping around the bar and gave every indication she might sit on it unless warned off. Skye also had to learn to keep her distance when the axe was being used but not before I clipped her once by axident, right between the eyes. Fortunately, it was only a glancing blow, but she still carries the scar and it certainly speeded up the teaching process! Even so, she had to be clobbered with the heel of the scythe a time or two before she learned to keep clear of that dangerous tool. She never did learn to stay far enough back of the horses on the trail, even though she received the odd kick. She had to be tied up when mowing was in progress as there was always the chance she would see a mouse in front of the cutter bar and chase it—with disastrous results.

Now, of all the animals on the farm, the most useless is Skye, the 15-year-old who no longer tries to interrupt our projects in order to get a game going. The days are past when she can get her own way either by being very crafty or simply irresistible. These days poor Skye is totally deaf and spends her winters in the barn or tied in the corral, for her own safety. She would not hear a predator if one came after her, nor would she know enough to get out of the way of horses. She still gets enjoyment out of life and will be provided with juicy bones to gnaw on in the sun for as long as she lives. She thumps her tail enthusiastically whenever someone stops to pat her.

In her younger days she would "help" with all sorts of jobs by such acts as placing a throwing stick in a motor undergoing repair, or putting her toy on a mower cutter bar as it was being sharpened, so whoever was doing the work would have to cooperate by tossing it out of the way. She would then go running joyously after it and return for more. She used to chase grizzlies but became increasingly cautious as the years passed. She would bark savagely and go after them but after one refused to turn, she learned to get out of range. She heeled well on trips and loved to accompany us on all our mountain jaunts. Skye never cared for swimming and proved her absolute devotion to us by joining us when we were mad enough to immerse ourselves in lake water. Reluctantly she would retrieve if the weather was warm and the water not too fast. She even plowed through big breakers once, in an absolute frenzy of participation! Skye always refused to acknowledge she was tired and could see no reason why anyone else should be. She loved the social amenities such as shaking paws and could scarcely be stopped once she had started. Having been taught the trick and rewarded with food for doing it, she probably figured shaking paws produced the tasty morsels. During the winter and spring of 1969-70, she kept the deer from the tender young apple trees and has also acted as a guard at gateways from time to time. Most of all, however, Skye has earned her keep by winning and giving love.

Last but not least, there are our two gentle and friendly barn cats over which all visitors to our place lavish great excesses of admiration for their beauty. Dumbo and Cealy are both tortoiseshells and in winter their coats display long guard hairs which give them almost a Persian appearance, or so we are told. They spend a good deal of time on the verandah and only rarely make a forbidden foray into the living quarters. They don't need to as they are quite capable of charming their humans out to the verandah for the affection they so obviously enjoy!

Both cats have learned from kittenhood to tolerate being tied up at certain times of the year when tiny birds are hatching. They are set free at night to roam but, in the daytime are secured to their sleeping boxes in warm but shady spots near the house. People have told us they remind them of miniature Eskimo sled dogs lying asleep in the sun!

19

"People-Watching" in the City

Whenever we make a foray "outside" we are amazed that
people can stand to live the way they do, much as folks from
the "civilized" world, with all its conveniences and
recreational facilities, express astonishment at the degree to
which we enjoy our life style.

We were doing business and visiting people in Victoria
and, after sight-seeing in the city, travelled by bus up
Vancouver Island to a small town called Parksville where
Jack's mother lives alone in a mobile home. We stayed with
her for several days. Susan spent a lot of her time across the
road where a family had ponies. We have five horses of our
own but she had been away from them for a few days, and the
ponies "took her home".

Leaving Parksville we travelled to Comox where air force
jets split the air with deafening thunder and screaming
whines. We stayed overnight there with a friend and next
day crossed the Strait of Georgia by bus to Powell River and
down to Vancouver.

We had some business to attend to in the big city as well as
some pleasures. We saw a couple of movies and spent a
noisy day at the Pacific National Exhibition. The most
attractive show there as far as Susan and I were concerned
was the horse show. We spent a day in Stanley Park and
looked at the animals in the zoo. The killer whale, Skana,

splashed water on us as we watched her doing several interesting tricks.

There were also a couple of shows which were absolutely free. Returning to our hotel one evening, we were riding in the stern end of a bus when we witnessed an incident which made us laugh. A large and determined female passenger who had been seated midway along the bus rose and lurched her way to the front, coming to a halt on one of the steps directly in front of the door just as the bus came to a stop for an intersection. The woman's bulk effectively blocked the driver's view of the street on the right, so he asked her to move. She replied snappishly that she had every right to stand there. The driver then allowed as how he was paid by the hour and didn't really care if they stayed there all night. Neither of them was about to give in, so the bus remained stationary through several complete light changes. Other passengers were beginning to mutter and the woman was starting to look a bit sheepish. The lady finally decided the driver was serious, so she slunk back to a seat and the bus moved off!

Since we have so little opportunity in the regular course of our lives to do so, we find *people-watching* is the greatest entertainment imaginable. This particular visit to the mainland city took place several years back when flower children roamed the streets of Vancouver. We saw lots of them, sprawling in doorways and on the Courthouse steps like seals basking on boulders in the sun!

Not all of them were taking it easy. Down by the beach where we had sat on a log to enjoy the evening harbor scene, five shabbily dressed hippies single-filed past us to an old partly wrecked small craft, upside down at the water's edge. They gathered round it, displaying great zeal at the prospect of launching it.

They began heaving and hauling on the heavy, waterlogged 10-footer, trying to drag it up on the sand in order to drain it. They then turned it over and pushed it into the water. It rode heavily about 20 feet before turning to lie broadside in the troughs in the changing tide which capsized it, spilling its passengers into the water. They righted it and hauled it out once more while one of the sailors kept calling for a can to bail with.

The next "voyage" saw just one longhair in the boat, the others content to give him a good push. He tried futilely to paddle with his hands but the sea soon turned the boat so that it lay into the swells and filled with water. He jumped out and as he was trying to manoeuvre the craft toward shore, a large wave lifted it, pushed it forward to hit the hippy in the chest, knocking him backwards into the cold water.

They gave up on the boat then but further along the beach, discovered a log which one fellow managed to launch. Once it was in deep water, he climbed aboard, but was promptly bucked off. The boat was given one final try but after yet another dunking, they all picked up their clothes and single-filed back in the direction they had come. After we dried our tears of laughter, we too continued on our way.

City folks probably get their share of surprises from us as well. We got some funny looks one time as we walked in from Vancouver International Airport after getting tired of waiting for a bus. Susan found the longest part of the journey was the length of Oak Street Bridge, which seemed to stretch into eternity. It wasn't the walk, but the proximity of the speeding cars, the smell and, worst of all, the lack of oxygen that bothered us.

One thing about city folks I cannot abide is their habit of tossing garbage out on the streets. Cigarette boxes are thrown casually from car windows and all too often a bottle is flung to the side of the road from a passing vehicle. They don't leave this tendency behind them when they enter our world, either. Some people seem unable to go anywhere without leaving a trail of garbage behind them, as though they are afraid of losing their way on the return trip if they haven't got their junk to follow. Even way out in the boondocks, where there is only the occasional hunter, we come across campsites marked with empty cans, paper bags and cigarette packages. I don't see why these uncaring persons can't either burn these items or carry them away and dispose of them decently. And I don't mean by dumping them in the nearest body of water, either. If they had room to carry bottles, cans and other things into the wilderness, they can surely carry them out empty. Even Trumpeter Trail, which is not often travelled, is littered with discarded cigarette boxes.

When we make a visit to the flower meadows on Trumpeter Mountain or the golden sandy beach at Junker Lake, we are very disturbed to come across a pile of rusting cans. It makes me unhappy to realize people will visit Tweedsmuir Park to enjoy the spectacular view of Talchako Mountain and mark their passage with refuse. If only they would leave nothing behind but their tracks!

Film instructions and chemical-backed papers tossed carelessly aside survive floods, snow, horses' hooves, bear paws and fallen leaves for many months. Tins last for years and bottles break, creating hazards for animals and human users of the wilderness. Glass can also act as a potential source of fire when it reflects the rays of the sun.

Even though we were living at Lonesome Lake long before the park was re-drawn to include us within its boundaries, we don't consider we own any more than the 160 acres which comprise Fogswamp Farm. We do not think of the rest of the area surrounding us as ours except in the way any animal thinks of its total environment as home.

Wherever we go we consider trees are home, much as an otter feels at home in water, even if it is in a bathtub. We are not fighting Nature when we clear some land of its trees. We are not struggling with the forest, we are merely changing the type of plant which will grow on that piece of ground. We feel fiercely protective towards the area that has been home throughout our lives. How many people just visiting the area for a short period could have such strong feelings about it?

It was a relief to finish up what we had to do in Vancouver and head for home. We left after searching in the rain for the Northland Navigation boat, Northland Prince, finally locating her just 15 minutes before she was due to sail, although she actually remained at the dock several hours more, loading freight.

When we disembarked at Bella Coola 24 hours later, it was raining as it had most of the voyage. We hadn't been able to see much of the rail except floating garbage all the way along the Inside Passage route. The stewards on the ship added to the mess after each meal, gathering all the paper napkins and tossing them out the portholes. All except the Turners', which were tucked away to keep them out of the sea!

We were to fly to Lonesome Lake on a Wilderness Airlines Cessna 185 the next day, but there was filthy weather until late that afternoon when the fog lifted a little. We had some 10-foot plywood for a boat and we wanted flown with us. The airline personnel told us we would have to cut it in half in order to be able to put it on the Cessna's spreader bars. Some unforeseen problems then came up and they could not locate a plane for us. Later they informed us the air was too turbulent to fly plywood on any craft. Eventually they flew us in to Lonesome Lake in the Stinson which was so small we had to leave the plywood and much of our other stuff behind. We were unhappy about the plywood because splitting it in half meant patching the bottom of the projected boat. Besides, Jack had to pack it in on his back after all, something we had hoped to avoid by chartering the plane.

The rain had stopped by the time we got home and we thought it was going to freeze that night. As evening came on, a dense ground fog spread itself protectively over our fields. It lay silent and unmoving until the rising sun warmed its back. Thus awakened, it rose, stretched, gathered itself and hurried off as though it had important business to attend to.

* * * * *

20

Williams Lake, February 20, 1976

Back to the bright lights from the Turner territory, I am
having a difficult time relating to all the big town amenities
in quite the same way I did a week ago. I've had an unforgettable experience and my perception is forever altered in
some respects because of it. I find myself contantly running
"memory tapes" of everything I've observed over the past
while.

The Turner family makes no open display of their deep
affection for one another but it is implicit in everything they
do, the small courtesies they show one another and the ever-
present vein of teasing that flows between them.

I had watched them closely and saw how well Trudy and
Jack work together, like tandem horses performing a job.
Susan spends a lot of time working with her mother and
there is a camaraderie between them that is a joy to see.
They poke fun at one another more like a pair of sisters than
mother and daughter. There seems to be no tension in the
household and the overall impression is of amicable
adaptation to one another's wishes and needs.

These are not heroic people although at first they seem to
be. There are no more dangers here for people with
knowledge of their surroundings and who keep their wits
about them than in the cities. Perhaps fewer, in fact. It gives
one a new perspective to sit in their kitchen, miles from
civilization, where wild animals supposedly roam around

looking for someone to eat, and listen to a radio broadcast telling of a sniper shooting at townhouses in North Toronto!

Agreed, they are living a life only a minority of people would choose. But it is not extraordinary to do as one wants. This is their choice and it is easy to see they thoroughly enjoy it.

The Turners practice what they preach about conservation. On their beloved Fogswamp Farm everything which can be re-cycled or re-used, is. Even the dust from the power saw is gathered and kept dry in readiness for use as soft bedding when a cow is calving. Nature is encouraged to work for the people who work with it and every living thing benefits. Killing is a miserable but necessary part of running a farm and the two-legged residents of Fogswamp feel very strongly about using every possible part of any creature they are forced through necessity to kill. Even the predators are understood to do their killing from need rather than for sport. Trudy has no particular dislike for carnivores. She feels man is a meat eater too and before he invented rifles, took his meat in a pretty cruel way. "I admit to feeling angry toward the predator which hurts a helpless calf but in the attacker's mind, that was his dinner staked out there on a chain. In any case, I only feel vengeful towards the particular beast that did the job, not the whole species," Trudy says.

She feels that man kills things for less reason than any other carnivore. Killing an animal which is causing a lot of trouble or which you need for food is justifiable but it is another matter to kill a bear, for example, just for the pleasure of being able to brag about having slain a monstrous creature with a high powered rifle...just before the unfortunate animal was able to make good its escape over a log.

"When a wolf makes a kill there is precious little left besides some hair, scraps of bone and some stomach contents. Cougars also utilize their kills efficiently. Man frequently kills simply for fun, taking out nothing but a trophy," Trudy comments sadly.

No one at Fogswamp even carries firearms in the bush from the first week in January to April 1. In 1976 there was only one bear track seen after the first of November. They don't carry a gun at all if horses are being ridden, for the

246

horses will either scare any wild animal away or can outrun it.

The family at Fogswamp wants and deserves no sympathy for the isolation, constant hard work, battles against the elements or deprivation of all the so-called conveniences. The Turners have no television, no phone to the outside world, no central heating, no medical or dental facilities. They can't go to a movie or a night club in the evening or run down to the corner store.

On the other hand, they don't have to put up with TV commercials; the phone doesn't ring at awkward moments; their heat costs nothing but the work of chopping wood; their water contains no unpleasant tasting chemicals; there are no automobile fumes (although they occasionally get the smell of industrial pollution sweeping down the valley), their electric bills are non-existent, and they take good care of themselves so they stay in remarkably good health.

In addition they enjoy incredible beauty anywhere they choose to look. Their home-grown beef steaks and roasts, fresh fruits and vegetables are incomparable. Susan and Trudy occasionally work together (during daylight hours) at the sewing machine, making their own clothes and other items. The iron, naturally, must be heated on the stove. The family enjoys music through their battery-operated stereo and the radio, and they own an extensive library which is in constant use. They delight in observing natural phenomena and are able to watch Mother Nature's show through all its daily and seasonal changes.

The Turners have a profound faith in the laws of Nature and appear to accept the existence of some sort of overall plan in the ordering of the world but that is about the extent of their religious beliefs.

Their cozy home is adorned with such unique articles as gnarled door handles, unusual furniture created by utilizing the natural configurations of trees, branches and roots and there is even a revolving stool, with a beautifully grained burl top, and tables supported by the graceful strength of a root. Their chairs are not only comfortable but aesthetically pleasing. These are constructed from branches especially chosen to provide the necessary curves, the seats and backs being laced with strips of cowhide with the hair still on. The overall feel of the home is of snugness and attractiveness with all its space well utilized. It is filled with the com-

247

panionship of people who share work and interests and who respect one another. It is a house of love.

Jack came from a background where the family was mutually concerned about one another. He has a deeply ingrained sense of responsibility and expresses his devotion to his family in practical ways.

Trudy's childhood was not a very warm one, although she admires her parents' achievements. Her relationship with her brothers is friendly but not close. Stanley, five years her elder, and John, almost three years older, both left home when Trudy was quite young and a great deal of responsibility devolved on her. There is still a lot of work in her life but the spirit of cooperation in which it is tackled takes the edge off the unpleasant aspects of it.

All during the winter there is the constant necessity to keep firewood on hand and to replenish the water supply daily. There is always stock to be fed and milked and the swans to be fed. The Turners walk five miles a day for approximately 100 days each winter on the latter job—500 miles annually. They have missed only two or three days over the past 20 years.

In addition, there are the constant jobs of general housework, getting meals and mending clothes. During the winter, too, a great deal of meat is put down for use during the warm months of the year. As soon as there are signs of impending thaw, the job of canning what is left of the fresh meat must commence.

Spring is a very busy time of year when new land is opened up and cleared, fences are repaired, manure is spread on the ground and seeds are planted.

When summer arrives the jobs of swan- and stock-feeding are eliminated as these creatures can then forage for themselves. There's still plenty to do, though, with priorities falling to weeding the garden, picking, canning and haying.

In May there is a special project. This is the cutting of more than 20 cords of wood for Mr. and Mrs. Gordon Corbould who run a lodge 12 miles from where the road meets the trail. The Turners thus show their appreciation for the fact he brings their mail in that far, provides truck transportation of supplies to that point and for the overnight accommodation the Corboulds hospitably extend. Since the Turners get a great deal of mail at a time, it is helpful for them to have a place where they can go through the

248

correspondence and write replies to some of it immediately.

Ever since the original book about the Edwards family was published there has been mail for both families from people all over the world. This has been especially true since an excerpt from the book is contained in American and Canadian schoolbooks. Some of the letters they receive are downright fawning while others express envy. There are requests from folks who want to come and visit and these almost invariably address Jack and Trudy by their first names as though they had known them all their lives. This is an aspect which has always bothered Trudy to some extent for she feels her dignity is broached when total strangers take such liberties. It is hard for her to understand that people who have read the book tend to come away from it with the feeling that they *have* grown to know the Edwards and Trudy very well. Some letters ask for reams of detailed information which would entail days or weeks to compile. There used to be hundreds of letters in every mail. Far too many to reply to without robbing themselves of the time they require to keep the place going, to say nothing of the expense of postage.

A surprising number of people appear to want to get away from cities, judging from the correspondence. Many of them even express a willingness to sell their homes and possessions so they can emulate the pioneers. These people are eager to try to live in this manner but many of them are simply not mentally or physically prepared for the inconvenience and hard work it involves and just couldn't make a go of it.

There are compartmented shelves in the Edwards' kitchen, built at the time when letters were arriving in vast numbers. It resembles a miniature post office. Letters still arrive there, addressing Trudy as though she is a small girl. Readers have felt the impact of her powerful personality and are curious to know more about her.

At any rate, when one's mail comes in only four times a year, it gets dealt with a little differently than when the postman delivers it to the door. To repay the Corboulds for all their kindnesses, Jack, Trudy and Susan put in about six days' work, with Trudy and Jack falling and limbing the trees while Susan helps load the truck and pile the wood near the lodge. Twenty days out of every year are taken up with the job of getting the mail.

On the fun side of the ledger, the Turners get a terrific

amount of enjoyment just from exploring their surroundings. Highlights of the year are the mountain hiking trips when they camp overnight, spending two or three days overall. Occasionally they take the horses to the hard beach at Junker Lake, where Trudy and Susan relish racing their horses. This excursion is most often in connection with a regular pack trip. The entire family enjoys reading and listening to records while Trudy adds painting and carving to her activities. Every so often there will be a musical evening when Trudy agrees to regale them with some Scottish music on her violin. She learned to play this instrument from her father who taught himself during the long winter evenings of his first few years alone on his preemption (at least he had no one to complain about sour notes) and although he played mostly hymns and western tunes, Trudy purchased instruction sheets and music for Scottish melodies and the family looks forward to hearing her perform the gay tunes. All three members of the family have skill and interest in creative writing and use much of their spare time in that pursuit.

Reviewing what had been talked about during my short but never-to-be-forgotten visit, I recalled the game we'd played one evening after supper as we all sat around the table. I wondered if there was anything at all the Turners would alter in life or if there was anything they considered a genuine hardship.

Announcing that I was a fairy godmother, I told them I was in the position to grant two wishes to each of them. I could give them anything they wished to add to their situation (cost to be, of course, of no consequence) and I could eliminate from their life one unwanted component.

Their responses were illuminating. Jack displayed absolutely no hesitation whatsoever in making his selection. He'd like a helicopter, please! He felt it would not only be useful for such mundane chores such as bringing in mail and supplies but, more important, would make frequent mountain trips more feasible.

He didn't delay very long in selecting what he would eliminate, either. "Summer tourists", he replied grimly. It is not that Jack dislikes people, but the Turners' apprehension in regard to fires which campers invariably light is extreme and with good reason. There is danger not only to their home and their stock, but their very lives. Beyond the fact it makes good sense to fear conflagration in their isolated situation, a subliminal memory may act as an additional influence on Trudy.

When she was just six months old, the cabin in which she was born burned to the ground. Everything except the clothes the family was wearing was lost. Since it was late October, and almost evening, it was necessary to use Ralph Edwards' original tiny earth-floored cabin as a home for five people for the approaching winter. The day after the fire some essential items were gathered from an unoccupied trapper's cabin. Very little was salvageable from the ashes of their home but the citizens of Bella Coola extended generous assistance as soon as they heard of the disaster. It was a desperately hard and miserable winter nevertheless and may well add to Trudy's awareness of the ever-present danger of fire.

The Turners have also had unforgettable experiences with people who come into their sensitive environment and display incredibly little sense in building campfires. Besides anxiety about fire, there are other prejudices tourists have fostered in the hearts of those whose livelihood depends on certain conditions remaining stable. Gates are important on a farm. When they are open they are generally that way for a reason. When closed, it is crucial they remain so. All too often, careless visitors have wandered around the property and left gates in positions other than the way they were found. This has resulted in damage to the garden and to the stock by allowing them to either reach food they should not, or closing them off from water.

Another aggravation has been the tendency of tourists to use boats and rafts which do not belong to them. Sometimes these have been damaged and in one instance a boat representing a huge investment in work and materials was left to go down the river where it smashed. There is, of course, the additional time and work involved in carrying supplies across rough terrain when a boat should have made the job easier and faster. The Turners' cabin at Stillwater was broken into and food stored for their overnight mail trips was gone when they arrived. For all these reasons, Jack felt he could do very well without the thoughtless, irresponsible summer tourist.

Susan's first selection from civilization's endless bounty was a library. She then thought it over and decided that since cost was no object, she'd go hog wild and put her order in for a huge, successful horse ranch where she would raise nothing but winners. Her dream barns and equipment were marvellously extravagant. She eventually came down to earth and confessed what she'd really add was a reliable radiophone service. Susan has encountered great difficulties in applying for jobs for the summer because her application has to be in ridiculously early in order to allow time for a reply to be received and plans made to leave the valley.

She elected to eliminate the sparse mail service, particularly in winter, on many of the same grounds. There may be other reasons for Susan's emphasis on communication, judging by some of the teasing that was directed her way and the swift rise of color in cheeks that definitely know how to blush!

When the questions were put to Trudy, she chose to have electricity added to her way of life. She did not plan to use this utility for anything beyond lighting and a refrigerator. Trudy tends to get a bit testy at suppertime when people get in the way of the lamp and throw shadows on what she is trying to see at the stove. She can often be seen checking the contents of a pot by flashlight!

As to what Trudy would eliminate—she opted for food shortages. To accomplish this, she would have wide, productive fields full of lush hay and would no longer have to fight the river for every square foot.

No one, to my everlasting bewilderment, even mentioned eliminating the little house standing out in the field, to which one has to make one's way in time of need, despite weather and darkness!

I remember the mixed feelings when my time at Fogswamp was coming to an end. At least, we were all under the impression that arrangements had been made for a plane to come in and take me out.

In a short span of time I felt I'd made friends who would always remain dear to me. We'd talked and talked. We'd walked and walked! We had exchanged opinions and ideas, verbalized dreams and revived memories.

On my next-to-last morning, I awoke early, listening for Trudy's footsteps as she came from the house to let me know breakfast was ready. I'd always tried to save her the entire trip but as usual I dozed off and just managed to call out "good morning" as she crossed Bear Bath Creek. It had been agreed I could "kidnap" Susan who wanted to come out with me and visit in Black Creek until it was time for her to take up her summer job at Lone Butte. On February 17, figuring we'd not be there for the actual day, Trudy baked a 17th birthday cake for her daughter and we all celebrated.

Conversation that evening turned to astrological signs and their meanings but none of us being very knowledgeable on the subject we didn't get far. The Turners celebrate all three birthdays within a period of just more than one month, but each has a different sign. Jack follows his Aquarius daughter by just three days but that makes him a Pisces while Trudy is an Aries, marking her birthday on March 30.

Before leaving Fogswamp, there was one impertinent question I had steeled myself to ask. I just had to know! One evening as Trudy had been making biscuits for supper, my eye had been caught by the imposing size of the rolling pin she was using. On learning Jack had carved the outsize implement for her, I couldn't help but wonder if he'd ever had reason to regret making it of such generous proportions. He assured me it had never yet been used in combat!

The morning of the 18th, after going down to visit and feed the swans, we all spent most of the afternoon stamping our feet in the cold and waiting for the expected plane to come in and take Susan and me to Anahim Lake. We waited in vain.

There was a brief flash of excitement when an aircraft actually landed on Big Lagoon that afternoon but it was the charter from Bella Coola coming to take out some Edwards beef. The pilot promised to remind the Wilderness Airline pilot at Anahim Lake that there were passengers waiting. By 5 o'clock we could only hope the other pilot would be able to reach him with the message. As we had no way of knowing when to expect the plane to arrive, we went home.

The morning of the 19th dawned with little sign of sun. The clouds were glued tightly to the mountaintops and we all scanned the sky to estimate if there was the mile visibility we knew was necesssary before anyone would fly in. At swan-feeding time, Jack, Susan and I headed out the trail with Susan leading Lucky who was loaded with bedding and the gear we were taking with us.

Trudy, who had stayed behind to look after the stock, had promised to give her mother a hand in the Edwards barn that afternoon since everyone at The Birches was busy wrapping beef. It was Trudy's intention to bring lunch down to us—steak and salt, she promised.

While Jack carried on to the "swannery", Susan and I ensconced ourselves on the mountainside, just a little up the bank from the lake opposite the hangar. We built a fire and huddled around it trying to keep reasonably warm in the 26°F weather. Trouble was, wherever it was warm, it also was smoky. Where the smoke wasn't, neither was there heat! We spent an hour or two circling the blaze and rambling off through the bush collecting fuel. At one point while Susan was over at her grandmother's house trying to find out if there had been any further radiophone contact with the airline, I heard a plane. Then the sound faded. Susan had started to rush out of the Edwards house when she first heard the sound but soon realized it was only a scheduled plane. However, to tease me, she demanded to know what on earth I thought I was doing, destroying our source of heat!. We rebuilt the fire and got it going nicely again by the time Trudy arrived. Susan had asked me a little earlier if I realized there wouldn't be plates to eat off. Knowing Trudy, I had of course taken her quite literally and was expecting salt and steak—no more, no less.

That steak was tender, flavorful, grilled over a wood fire, salted and eaten outdoors in cold crisp air, in good company.

Then the weather began to get miserable. It hailed briefly, then snowed. When we heard a plane, neither of us touched a stick of wood from the fire. We just craned our necks skyward. The small plane circled and began to descend. It headed off toward the end of Big Lagoon, through the narrow opening between the hills and on into the main body of Lonesome Lake. And that was that. It just vanished. As the afternoon wore on, our patience (especially Lucky's) wore thin, Lucky had been giving us strange looks for hours.

The conversation between Susan and me revolved around "ifs". The horrible truth was there was no way at all to be certain anyone "out there" had the slightest notion *we* wanted to get out! We gave up and went home again. For the second time I unpacked my sleeping bag and re-made my bed.

The morning of the 20th, I rebelled and decided I was darned if I was going through the performance again. My bed was going to stay made until we got definite word from Mrs. Edwards that she had reached the airline and completed a clear two-way conversation with them and they were coming in for certain at a particular time. Following a leisurely breakfast, we were idly chatting around the table when Susan, who had been out to the barn, charged in and said: "I don't know if it's ours or not but a plane just landed at the hangar."

I leaped at the phone and called Mrs. Edwards who confirmed that a plane was at that very minute taxiing to the hangar to meet us. Talk about fast action! I raced for my little cabin, rolled my bedding faster than ever before, grabbed all my bits and pieces, slung the pack over my shoulders and set off alone at close to a run. We emerged one by one onto the frozen expanse of Big Lagoon, about a hundred feet apart, each of us having taken off the instant we were ready. The gear was quickly loaded aboard the small plane, we made our farewells and Susan and I boarded.

No question about it, I thought with satisfaction as the plane's motor warmed up, it's been a magnificent seven day physical fitness course. The first time I travelled Trumpeter Trail it took a labored forty-five minutes. Today, with a plane waiting at the hangar, I had negotiated it in under twenty-five minutes and still had breath left for conversation!

The pilot circled and banked as we left. The last I saw was a small group of tiny figures standing in the middle of a vast area of white ice, surrounded by forest. Trudy, Jack, Mrs. Edwards and John waved us goodbye as we began our bumpy flight out of the splendid wilderness called "home" by some very remarkable people... and some unforgettably beautiful white swans.

A sequel to "The Crusoe of Lonesome Lake"

Ralph Edwards
OF LONESOME LAKE

THE
COMPLETE
BIOGRAPHY
OF THE
CRUSOE
OF
LONESOME
LAKE

by Ed Gould

Author Ed Gould continues the story of this remarkable man and his pioneer life in the Bella Coola Valley.

288 pp 5½x8½ 15 color photos and 50 black and white
Hancock House   ISBN 0-919654-74-6
Printed in Canada